THE *BetterWay* TO

Create BASIC SCRAPBOOKS

Michele Gerbrandt

BETTERWAY BOOKS
Cincinnati, Ohio

BOOK DIRECTORS	*Michele & Ron Gerbrandt*
EXECUTIVE EDITOR	*Kerry Arquette*
EDITOR	*MaryJo Regier*
ART DIRECTOR	*Andrea Zocchi*
CRAFT DIRECTOR	*Erikia Ghumm*
ASSOCIATE EDITOR	*Kimberly Ball*
IDEA EDITOR	*Janetta Wieneke*
PHOTOGRAPHER	*Ken Trujillo*
PHOTO STYLIST	*Sylvie Abecassis*
CONTRIBUTING WRITERS	*Laurie Connolly, Brooke Fluette, Carol Kauder, Deborah Mock, Jill A. Rinner, Lori Elkins Solomon, Patti Swoboda, Maureen Taylor, Anne Wilbur, and Memory Makers readers*
CONTRIBUTING PHOTOGRAPHERS	*Liz Campanella, Marc Creedon, Christina Dooley, Brenda Martinez*
CONTRIBUTING DESIGNERS	*Susha Roberts, Karen Roehl*
CONTRIBUTING ARTISTS	*Brandi Ginn, Ann Kitayama, Carol Snyder*
EDITORIAL SUPPORT	*Dena Twinem*

The BetterWay to Create Basic Scrapbooks.
Copyright ©2004 Memory Makers Books.
All rights reserved.

Published by Betterway Books, an imprint of F+W Publications, Inc.
4700 East Galbraith Road, Cincinnati, OH 45236
Phone 1-800-289-0963
First edition. Manufactured in the United States of America.

08 07 06 05 04   5 4 3 2 1

A catalog record for this book is available from the Library of Congress
at http://catalog.loc.gov.

Memory Makers Books is the home of *Memory Makers*, the scrapbook magazine dedicated to educating
and inspiring scrapbookers. To subscribe, or for more information, call 1-800-366-6465.
Visit us on the Internet at www.memorymakersmagazine.com

THIS BOOK BELONGS TO

_____

This book is dedicated to my husband, Ron,
and our three kids, Anna, Sasha and Daniel.
Thank you for providing me with endless opportunities
for wonderful memories in my scrapbooks.

Contents

16

41

57

80

113

THE GERBRANDT'S

OUR FAMILY

DANIEL, AGE 7
MICHELE, AGE 36
SASHA, AGE 9½
RON, AGE 38
ANNA, AGE 12

2002

Introduction

Welcome to the world of creative scrapbooking! There seems to be at least one person in each family who always has a camera in hand. She's the one recording the three-legged races at Fourth of July picnics and that special moment when birthday wishes are made and candles blown out. She understands that the rich and most rewarding moments in our lives are worth reliving through photos, carefully preserved in albums. If you are holding this book in your hands, chances are that we are describing you.

Contemporary scrapbooking is the art of arranging photos and journaling in a photo-safe environment. Scrapbook pages can be simple or complex. They may include memorabilia such as movie ticket stubs, theater programs or sports tickets. Pages can be decorated with stickers, pens, embossed designs and much, much more. With the wide and growing range of products available, only time and imagination limit today's scrapbooker.

If you are new to the art of scrapbooking, you may be confused about where and how to begin. This book has been created to set you on the path to a lifetime of scrapping enjoyment. We will address questions such as: What do I need to get started? How do I find supplies? What does "photo safe" mean and how do I identify safe albums and products? What should I include in my journaling? There are instructional pages that will guide you through the process of sorting and organizing photos and laying out beautiful scrapbook pages. Both new and seasoned scrapbookers will draw inspiration from the page ideas of *Memory Makers* readers and our talented staff.

Creating an album can be a very rewarding experience. I discovered contemporary scrapbooking in 1992 and it has changed my life, opening up new worlds of possibilities. I continue to learn and grow as a scrapbooker day by day and year by year. I am so pleased that you have decided to join me on this journey. Enjoy creating your albums. You have so many special memories to preserve and stories that are just waiting to be told.

Michele

Michele Gerbrandt
Founder of *Memory Makers*® magazine

> SCRAPBOOKING BONDS, TRANSFORMS AND CAN HELP HEAL PEOPLE.
> —*Michele*

The history of scrapbooking

A scrapbook is magic. It captures and cradles life's most precious moments. Through photographs, memorabilia, journaled thoughts and stories, scrapbooks evoke our fondest memories and allow us to relive daily and once-in-a-lifetime experiences.

While the earliest forms of scrapbooking can be traced back to the 16th century, modern scrapbooking really began with the invention of photography in 1826. That's when a Frenchman by the name of Nicéphore Niépce first captured an image on a sheet of metal. Thirteen years later the first camera became available to the public. In the mid-1800s, the popularity of portrait photography received an infusion when a method was discovered which made it possible to make multiple prints. Today's scrapbookers are walking in the well-tread footsteps of photography's Golden Age, set down more than one hundred years ago!

LOOKING BACK

1598 An author refers to gathering "words and approved phrases...to make use as it were a common place booke [sic]."

1709 John Locke, a philosopher, publishes his *New Method of Making Common-place Books*.

1769 William Granger introduces a book that includes extra blank pages. It starts a hobby known as "extra illustrating" books.

1798 Lithography, a printing technique which fixes images on a stone or metal plate using ink-absorbent and ink-repellent vehicles, is invented.

1800s Young women keep friendship albums filled with hair weavings and writings.

1837 Godefroye Englemann invents chromolithography, a process of lithography in colors from a series of plates.

1859 Card photographs known as cartes de visite come to the United States.

1860s Mass production of advertising cards for companies and products begins.

1867 John Jerrard of London calls himself a dealer in photographs and scrap prints of every description for albums and scrapbooks.

My Nana's
Wedding portrait
Ann M. Baron
June 16th. 1938
Chester. P.A.

Preserving beloved wedding photos, whether they are contemporary photos or heritage photos, is a common thread that often brings people to scrapbooking.

I modeled my
wedding flowers
after Nana's.

1872 Mark Twain markets his self-pasting scrapbook.

1880 E.W. Gurley publishes *Scrapbooks and How to Make Them.*

1888 George Eastman sells the Kodak camera for amateur photographers under the slogan, "You push the button, we do the rest."

1945 Prizes offered for children's scrapbooks.

1970s Alex Haley's *Roots* spurs a resurgence of interest in family history.

1996 *Memory Makers®* magazine begins publication.

Scrapbooking today

Scrapbookers know the value of preserving memories. They understand that the pages they create are, and will be, cherished. By using carefully selected products, they ensure their albums will survive and become heirlooms. Future generations will open the scrapbooks and hear the voices of their creators. In learning about us, they will have a better understanding of themselves.

Modern scrapbooking has evolved as an understanding of those elements damaging to photos and memorabilia has emerged. Only in recent years have the terms "archival quality," "photo-safe," "lignin- and acid-free," and "buffered paper" become household words. Today's scrapbookers look for products bearing these labels, knowing the use of these products will create a safer environment and better preserve album contents. As scrapbooking has grown in popularity, more supplies and products have become available. Today, shoppers can choose from thousands of products, including stickers, stamps, papers, die cuts and pens, which open windows of creative opportunity.

SAFER SCRAPBOOKING PRODUCTS

- PVC-free plastic page protectors and memorabilia keepers: PVC releases fumes that destroy photos and paper.

- Permanent pigment inks: Other inks fade, bleed and spread.

- Photo-safe and acid-free adhesives: Other adhesives can damage photos.

- Acid- and lignin-free album pages and paper products: Acid and lignin cause photos and paper to degrade and discolor.

- Buffered paper: Buffered products help act as a barrier to prevent chemicals from contaminating paper and damaging photos and pages.

REMOVE PHOTOS FROM MAGNETIC ALBUMS

Sandwiched between the self-adhesive pages and plastic overlays, your photos will discolor, become brittle and deteriorate. Here are ways to remove photos safely:

- Remove photos by slipping a slender knife or dental floss beneath a corner to loosen it.

- To loosen photos that are firmly stuck to the page, try a commercial adhesive remover such as un-du's PhotoCare™ Solution. It removes smudges and adhesive residue safely from photos.

- If the album's plastic overlay is stuck to your photos, consult a conservator.

- Never force a photo from a page. If photos are truly stuck, consider investing in reprints rather than attempting to remove.

- Never use heat to loosen photos from a page.

Why do we scrapbook?

There are as many reasons to scrapbook as there are scrapbookers. Your reason for scrapbooking is as personal and unique as the album you are about to create. On the pages that follow, you will find a number of scenarios that bring people just like you to the rewarding hobby of scrapbooking.

1. DOCUMENT FAMILY HISTORY

Photos are a great way to document important family events as they unfold. Displayed within a scrapbook, they can be enjoyed each time the book is opened. Long after those in the images are gone, their faces remain familiar and journaled pages give voice to their hopes, dreams, fears and foibles.

2. TELL A STORY

Pictures tell stories that can be expanded upon through creative and concise journaling. Using photos as springboards, scrapbookers then fill in important information such as when and where a picture was taken and who appears in the image. But they can do much more. By recording snippets of conversation, jokes and contemplations, journaling can recreate the mood of events and bring the stories back to life.

Recipients of heritage photos and those fond of genealogical research often turn to scrapbooking because it provides the perfect harbor for preserving images and hard-found documentation together.

Bonnie Peacock, Sevierville, Tennessee

3. MAKE A GIFT

Show those you love how important they are and what their presence has meant in your life with a gift album. Gift albums may include photos of special times you have shared or may pay tribute to the scrapbook's recipient. Either way, a gift album is sure to be a cherished treasure.

4. GET PHOTOS ORGANIZED

If you're like most people, there's a box or drawer somewhere in your home devoted to a mess of random photos. Tucked away in that desk or dresser, or hidden in boxes under beds and in closets, they are all but forgotten. Creating a scrapbook is a great motivator to finally pull out your photos and put them in order.

5. ENJOY SOMETHING CREATIVE

Break out the scissors. Wade through reams of colored paper. Make a scrapbook that is fun, creative and uniquely your own. Scrapbooking lets your imagination run wild. You're preserving memories and at the same time stretching your artistic side. The sense of accomplishment you gain will be long lasting.

At one time or another, we all have a stockpile of unorganized photos just begging to be put in a scrapbook album to have their stories told.

6. HELP HEAL

A tragedy, whether it is suffering personal illness or the loss of a loved one, can leave you staggering with grief. When the pain has subsided, you may wish to scrapbook about your experience, your thoughts and feelings. Scrapbooking is a wonderful tool for reliving the good times and moving past those that are difficult. It can be extremely therapeutic.

Baby's first year bustles with rapid growth and change. Few parents can resist capturing those sweet little grins and miraculous "firsts" in a baby scrapbook album.

7. START A BABY ALBUM

The first tooth, the first word, the first step. Those baby days go by in a flash and you'll want to record all those special "firsts" in an album. A scrapbook featuring your children will bring back the smell of baby powder and the sound of "patty cake" hands. Later, your children will revel in their earliest adventures (and misadventures!).

8. MAKE NEW FRIENDS

New people are discovering scrapbooking daily. Scrapbookers gather at quilting-bee-like events called "crops." They attend large conventions and small workshops, gather in mountain and lakeside resorts and on cruise ships, and chat online. Wherever they meet, scrapbookers make new friends with whom they share their love of scrapbooking.

The future of scrapbooking

A handful of years ago creative scrapbooking was in its infancy. In intervening years, it has grown, matured, and gained in popularity. Today, more than 20 percent of American households have members who scrapbook and the hobby is gaining popularity worldwide.

Where once it was difficult to find scrapbook tools and supplies, now more and more stores are dedicating whole sections to meeting the needs of this craft audience. Across the nation, scrapbook stores are popping up, catering exclusively to scrapbookers' needs. Today's scrapbookers continue to push the envelope, exploring new ways to use the growing variety of available products and tools. You are part of this great movement to preserve life's memories. And your efforts will help define the future of this wonderful art form.

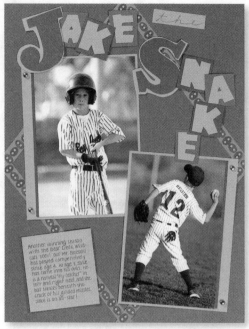

More and more scrapbookers are adding hardware to their scrapbook pages. Metal fasteners and eyelets are the latest craze to hit scrapbooking.

Photos MaryJo Regier, Littleton, Colorado

Wire is adding a new twist to scrapbooks with its hand-shaped versatility and its many colors.

Alexandra Bleicher, Chilliwack, BC, Canada

One of the most fun trends to come to scrapbooking is creative photo cropping. Silhouette cropping is just one of the many simple cropping techniques that can bring visual impact to your scrapbook pages.

Photos Tiare Smith Woods, Evanston, Illinois

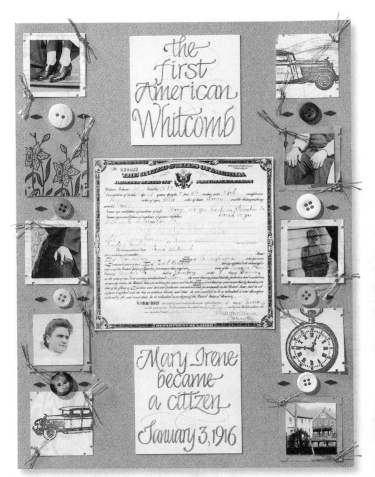

Creative photo cropping takes on many artistic forms—in this case a mosaic—which allows you to use many photos on one scrapbook page.

Veronique Grasset, Montreau, France

Baubles, in the form of buttons, and organic materials such as raffia are increasingly finding their way into scrapbook albums when a homespun look is desired. Beads and embroidery stitching are also perfectly at home on scrapbook pages.

Erikia Ghumm, Denver, Colorado
Photos Pennie Stutzman, Broomfield, Colorado

Heat embossed rubber stamping continues to grow in popularity with the increasing numbers of gorgeous stamp designs in countless themes and pigment inks and embossing powders in dazzling colors.

Joyce Schweitzer
Greensboro, North Carolina

AS YOU WISH

For Sasha's 9th Birthday, we had a Ceramics party at As You Wish in Boulder, Colorado. Sasha received a Birthday plate, that we now use for each family members Birthday! June 15, 2001

Tools & supplies

Most experienced scrapbookers feel like kids in a candy shop when visiting their local scrapbook or hobby store. But newcomers to the hobby can easily be overwhelmed, even intimidated, by the plethora of scrapbook supply choices available. If you've never been in a scrapbook store or the scrapbook section of a hobby store, prepare yourself to see shelves and shelves filled with adhesives, albums, die cuts, papers, pens, punches, stamps, stickers, templates and more. Some shoppers give in to temptation and scoop up goodies by the basketful, while others flee out the door as empty-handed as when they arrived.

Successful shopping for supplies involves planning and an understanding of your personal scrapbooking needs. In the following pages you'll learn how to select the tools and products needed to create lasting books. You'll discover ways to organize and care for your materials so they'll continue to perform year after year.

PURCHASING SUPPLIES IS JUST LIKE GOING TO THE GROCERY STORE. IT'S BEST TO START OUT WITH A LIST

–Michele

Building a scrapbook toolbox

You are probably wondering what you need to get started. Beginning any new hobby requires an investment. Scrapbooking is no different. While you may find some useful tools in your home utility drawer (see page 19), you will most likely need to purchase some basic supplies in order to begin creating albums.

CONSUMABLE SUPPLIES VS. NON-CONSUMABLE TOOLS

Consumable supplies are those products that will be used up and need to replenished over time. Non-consumable supplies are those tools that keep on giving and giving until they eventually break or wear out. With proper care, most non-consumable tools will last indefinitely! As you become more involved with scrapbooking, you will note a distinct difference between the two.

CONSUMABLE SUPPLIES

Adhesive remover

Die cuts

Ink pads

Photo-safe adhesives

Pigment pens and markers

Solid and patterned papers

Stickers

NON-CONSUMABLE TOOLS

Craft knife

Cutting mat (not shown)

Paper crimpers

Paper trimmer (not shown)

Punches

Rulers

Scissors

Shape cutters

Stamps

Templates

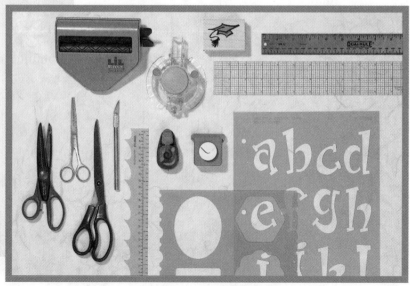

Tools you may already have

The majority of hobbyists who come to scrapbooking already have some basic craft tools they use regularly for other hobbies. Many of the supplies you will find useful in scrapbooking are already close at hand, such as a sturdy, sharp pair of scissors and a metal straightedge ruler. Before you go shopping for new items, check around the house for any of the following supplies to add to your beginner's toolbox.

TOOLS YOU MAY OWN

Adhesive remover

Craft knife and extra blades

Cutting mat

Graphing or grid ruler

Metal straightedge ruler

Photo-safe adhesives

Regular scissors

Removable artists tape

Small, sharp scissors

Tweezers

Tools you'll need

As your interest in scrapbooking grows, and as you are ready to explore new artistic challenges, you can slowly add to your scrapbooking toolbox. Let's take a look at the various tools and supplies that eventually end up in a scrapbooker's arsenal, starting with the most basic needs of any beginner.

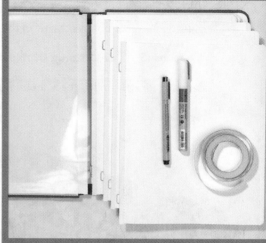

THE BEGINNER'S TOOLBOX

Album

Album pages

Black pigment pen

Page protectors

Photo-safe adhesive

INTERMEDIATE ADD-ONS

Colored paper

Corner rounder punch

Decorative rulers

Decorative scissors

Fancy and colored pens

Personal paper trimmer

Scrapbook magazines and
   idea books

Simple shape templates

COST-SAVING TIPS

BECOME A PREFERRED CUSTOMER Frequent shoppers may be rewarded with discounts. Some scrapbooking stores have punch cards that add up to steep savings based on the amount of goods purchased.

BUY IN BULK Many retailers offer quantity discounts on items such as paper, stickers and page protectors. Consider splitting the supplies with friends.

COMPARE PRICES Shop around, search catalogs and watch for sales in order to get the best bargains.

SUGGESTIONS FOR
THE EXPERIENCED

Alphabet and decorative
    stickers

Die cuts

Lettering and nested
    templates

Paper crimper

Patterned paper

Punches

Shape cutters

Stamps and ink pads

Vanishing ink pen

Vellum, mulberry, and
    other specialty papers

KEEP IT SIMPLE Great layouts aren't necessarily busy. A lot of imagination and a few products can create stunning pages.

MAKE A WISH LIST (*see page 39*) Before a gift-giving holiday, supply those who love you with a list of products you would like to receive. Be specific about manufacturers, colors, sizes and styles.

SHARE OR RENT TOOLS Rent tools from your local store, or crop with friends and share tools, conversation and laughter.

SWAP SUPPLIES Collect tools and supplies you no longer want and swap them with friends for products you need.

USE COUPONS Stores provide discount coupons in ads and fliers, which may cut the cost of your purchases by up to 50 percent.

USE YOUR COMPUTER Download free fonts and clip art or order supplies online at discount prices.

USE YOUR LOCAL LIBRARY Borrow books on art design or scrapbooking from your local library.

Using your tools & supplies

It's time to shop! But before you get started, take a few minutes to learn more about the scrapbook supplies and tools that are on the market. Understanding the products and their uses will make it easier for you to select precisely the items that will best suit your needs. Remember that all supplies you purchase should be safe for use with your photos and memorabilia (see page 10). Keep those archival issues in mind as your interest in scrapbooking and your number of tools and supplies grow.

POST BOUND

STRAP STYLE

ALBUMS

One of your first scrapbook purchases will be an album—the book in which you display your crafted pages. Albums come in various styles and sizes, ranging from 4 x 6" to 12 x 15". When choosing an album, consider the size and shape of your photos and memorabilia, as well as the style of book you wish to create. Newspaper clippings, greeting cards and large portraits, for example, may dictate a larger scrapbook while a small collection of photos may better be displayed in a smaller album. Make certain whichever album you select is an archival-quality environment for your photos and memorabilia. In addition, use only page protectors made of non-reactive, PVC-free plastic—such as polypropylene or polyester.

POST BOUND This album type features post screws in the album's binding that allow you to add or rearrange pages. Extension posts may also be purchased for further expansion. Most post-bound albums include a starter set of pages with refill pages and page protectors available separately. Some post-bound albums bind the page protectors into the album's posts rather than the page.

STRAP STYLE A strap-style album uses plastic straps woven through sturdy staples attached to pages or page protectors. The albums lie flat when opened, and facing pages lie close together, hiding the binding. Like three-ring and post-bound albums, this style lets you add or rearrange pages.

THREE-RING BINDER This style of album is expandable to the width of its spine. Its pages generally slide in and out of top loading page protectors mounted on the binder rings. Using separate sheets of paper for the front and back of each scrapbook page, you can easily change the order of the pages in the album. Look for cloth binders with acid-free cores and nonreactive adhesives.

SPIRAL A spiral-bound album is great for finite projects such as gift albums. They come with pages already bound in to them. If you have an ongoing project, however, look for a more expandable album style.

THREE-RING BINDER

SPIRAL

PAPER

Paper, an essential ingredient in creative scrapbooking, comes in hundreds of colors, patterns, textures and weights. To be photo-safe, paper should be pH neutral (acid-free) and lignin-free. Many varieties of paper are also buffered, which is preferable for scrapbooking projects. Not all vellums, mulberry, metallic or handmade papers are archivally safe and, as such, should not be allowed to directly touch photos and memorabilia. Paper is sold in single sheets, packets and booklets. Mix and match both to create a one-of-a-kind look in your album. Create punch art and select die cuts and stickers that work well with the colors of your papers and the themes of your photos.

TYPES OF PAPER

DECORATIVE OR PATTERNED PAPER Multi use paper that can tie pages together and support theme layouts; available in hundreds of different designs and patterns.

SOLID-COLORED PAPER Basic solid papers, available in hundreds of colors and a variety of weights, can be used alone or with decorative or patterned paper.

CARDSTOCK Sturdier paper that is available in a multitude of colors and patterns; especially useful for matting photos and making die cuts. Used as a base for pages in top-loading albums.

VELLUM Transparent paper great for decorative elements; can be drawn or printed upon and laid over pages for sheer effects.

SUEDE A leathery-looking paper available in a number of colors; useful for adding texture to pages that have hair, clothing, or animal themes.

Photos Chrissie Tepe, Lancaster, California

MULBERRY Papers with a heavy look of wood fiber; useful for pages calling for a natural, outdoorsy feel.

HANDMADE Reminiscent of old-fashioned, rough-textured paper, its fibers, confetti and other elements are visible; great for heritage pages and poetic layouts.

METALLIC Shiny, metallic papers—some holographic—available in many colors; useful for replicating page accents of metallic objects such as jewelry, eyeglasses, picture frames, candlesticks, cars, etc.

PENS

A pen is more than just a writing implement. It is an important scrapbooking tool. Only pigment pens should be used in scrapbooks. Pigment ink is lightfast, fade-resistant, waterproof and colorfast. The right pen can make writing a pleasure. The wrong pen can ruin a pretty page. So, before you buy your scrapbook pens, consider your writing style and project needs. Remember that getting used to any pen takes practice. If, after some time, you still don't feel comfortable with the tool, set it aside and move on. Eventually you'll find the pen that works best for you. To every person there is a pen and a tip for every purpose under the sun.

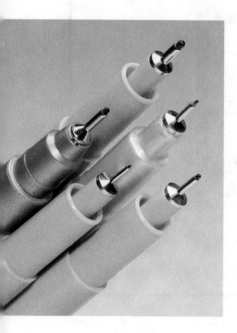

JOURNALING PENS Your first scrapbook pen should be a basic black pigment pen for journaling. These pens come with delicate, fine points as well as thicker point sizes. The best way to choose a journaling pen is to experiment. If your store has testers, try them. See how a pen feels in your hand. Try to buy an individual pen rather than a large set. Take it home. Get used to it and, if it feels as though it is right for you, invest in others that are similar.

DECORATIVE PENS When you're ready to experiment with more creative lettering, you'll want to invest in special decorative pens. These writing tools come in a variety of tips, from brush to bullet and calligraphy to chisel. Each decorative pen creates a different look. Experts advise beginners to stick to the bullet tip, a general-use pen that is good for a variety of decorative purposes.

PEN TYPE AND USES

SMALL BRUSH
Decorative lettering, creating thick and thin lines

SMALL CALLIGRAPHY
Decorative lettering, pen work, journaling

BULLET
Journaling, bold lettering, drawing and coloring in

SCROLL
Fancy letters, pen work, not for extensive journaling

CHISEL
Decorative lettering and embellishments

FINE POINT DRAWING AND WRITING
Journaling, detailed pen work

LARGE BRUSH
Decorative lettering, pen work, coloring in

LARGE CALLIGRAPHY
Decorative lettering, embellishments

 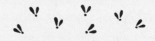

 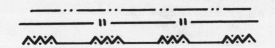

 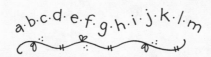 

Lettering created by Carol Snyder for EK Success

ADHESIVES

The word "adhesives" conjures visions of kindergarten class and white-paste projects. However, today's scrapbook adhesives are nothing like the goopy glues of the past. Modern scrapbookers have access to a wide range of glues and tapes that make it quick and easy to attach photos and memorabilia to pages. While the choice of adhesive often boils down to personal preference, scrapbookers should be certain to select products that are photo-safe and acid-free. Unsafe adhesives can damage photos, causing deterioration.

Adhesives are considered either "wet" or "dry". Each is right for different tasks. Because different adhesives require different types of application, it may take some experimentation to find the one that suits your needs.

HOW TO USE ADHESIVES

BOTTLED GLUE Bottled glue is more fluid than other scrapbook adhesives, and requires careful application. It dries slowly, but creates a strong bond between photo and paper. Overuse can buckle some types of paper; test it on a sample scrap first. This type of adhesive works well on small embellishments and three-dimensional objects such as buttons and sequins.

GLUE STICKS Glue sticks contain a thick, pasty adhesive that dries quickly and will not buckle paper. The sticks come in a variety of sizes. Consider using these to mount photos and large pieces of paper, journaling blocks and titles, as well as die cuts.

LIQUID GLUE PENS Glue pens come in a variety of pen tips. The pens dispense glue when pressed against paper. The pens are especially useful for adhering tiny pieces, such as punched shapes and hand-cut lettering, to a scrapbook page.

PHOTO SPLITS Photo splits are double-sided tape, precut into tiny pieces. Some splits are packaged inside of applicators. Other types of splits are sold in a roll with protective backing that must be peeled off before applying them to the page. Splits are especially useful for adding photo mosaics, photos, blocks of journaling or titles and paper embellishments to your scrapbook pages.

PHOTO TAPE Photo tape is two-sided tape that comes on a roll. Unlike splits, the tape is not pre-sectioned and therefore the scrapper may cut pieces of any size as needed. The tape comes with a protective backing that must be peeled away. Photo tape makes it easy to attach pocket pages and other large decorative elements or photos to your pages.

SELF-ADHESIVE FOAM SPACERS
These double-sided adhesives come in a variety of sizes and thicknesses and can be cut to add dimension to even the tiniest page accent.

TAPE ROLLERS Tape rollers are applicators that allow you to roll double-sided adhesive on paper. They are similar to photo tape, however they do not require you to strip off a protective backing. The most versatile of all adhesives, tape rollers can be used to mount photos, journaling blocks and titles, die cuts and paper embellishments. To dispense the adhesive, you roll the applicator across a page.

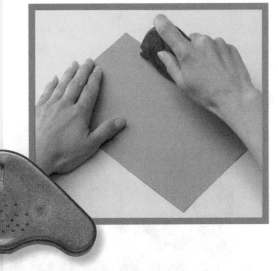

XYRON™ ADHESIVE APPLICATION MACHINE The Xyron is a machine through which you send your photos or paper and they become stickers with a peel-away backing. The Xyron works especially well for adhering vellum and punched pieces. Thermo-Web is another adhesive application product. It does not require the use of a machine.

CUTTING TOOLS

Cutting tools are an important part of any scrapbook toolbox. They are used for everything from creating mats and borders to cropping photos. The right cutting tool can make a job easier for tentative croppers. Every scrapbooker should own a pair of large and small straightedged scissors for general-purpose cutting. There are a number of other exceptional cutting tools on the market that will make cropping and creating even more fun.

DECORATIVE SCISSORS Decorative scissors come in many patterns and depths of cut. Some scissors have shallow teeth for creating tighter, smaller pattern cuts. Others have deep teeth for carving more extended, flowing designs. It may take practice to learn to successfully use decorative scissors, but it's worth the effort.

HOW TO USE DECORATIVE SCISSORS

- Draw a guideline on your paper where you plan to cut.

- Line up your blade slightly to the left of the penciled line so no markings will be visible (or on the line, if you use a vanishing ink pen).

- Steady your cutting arm by anchoring the elbow to your side. Use the other hand to turn the paper or photo as you cut. Do not turn the scissors.

- Starting halfway from the base of the blade, begin your cut.

- Use the longest strokes possible. Short, choppy strokes interrupt the scissors' pattern.

- Stop cutting before you reach the end of the blade.

- Flip the scissors over to achieve a varied scissor pattern.

- To create an uninterrupted pattern, carefully realign the blade after each cut, matching a portion of the cut pattern with the design on the blade.

- Use decorative scissors to create mats, decorative elements, crop photos, or make borders.

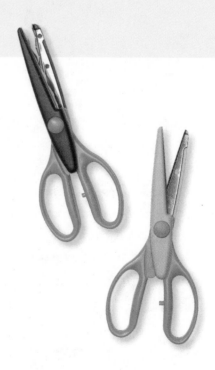

Valerie Brincheck for Fiskars, Inc.

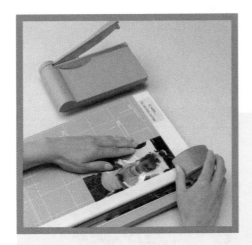

PERSONAL PAPER TRIMMERS Paper trimmers are perfect for making straight cuts and 90-degree angles. They come in a variety of sizes.

HOW TO USE A PAPER TRIMMER

- Place your index finger and thumb (or your entire hand) firmly on the photo or paper you wish to trim. With your other hand, bring down the handle, or slide down the blade, quickly and smoothly.

- Use smaller paper trimmers to cut mats or cleanly crop photos.

- Use larger trimmers such as a rotary disk trimmer for cutting photo enlargements, scrapbook papers, cardstock and corrugated paper.

SHAPE CUTTERS Shape blade cutters and nested templates are manufactured by a number of companies. They are useful when cropping photos, mats and journaling blocks into perfect shapes. Shape cutters can cut circles, ovals and many other simple shapes.

Photos Cheryl Rooney, Lakewood, Colorado

HOW TO USE A SHAPE CUTTER

- Determine the size of the circle you wish to cut and set the blade accordingly.

- Place the cutter so the center pin sits in the middle of the photo you wish to cut. Press the pin down firmly with one finger. With the other hand, guide the extension bar around in a circle. Apply even pressure until you have completed the revolution.

- Use a nested template such as a Colluzzle® to inexpensively cut a variety of shapes. Nested templates are transparent templates that can be placed over photos or paper. While firmly holding down the item you wish to cut, slip the blade tool into the narrow cutting channel. Allow the channel to guide your slice as you complete the pattern.

- Use shape cutters to crop photos or decorative elements such as die cuts or journaling palates.

TEMPLATES

Templates are stencil-like patterns made of plastic, sturdy paper or cardboard. They can be homemade or purchased and have a multitude of uses.

Templates come in a variety of sizes, shapes and themes including hearts, animals, simple geometric patterns, page borders and photo frames. With templates in hand, anyone can turn boxy, rectangular photos and mats into something special.

JOURNALING TEMPLATES
The circular coil of this journaling template makes it easy to follow the lines when adding words to the page.

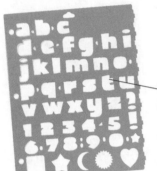

LETTER TEMPLATES
A chunky-style letter template adds energy to a go-getting page title.

SHAPE TEMPLATES
Two different sizes of oval templates were used to crop these photos.

DECORATIVE RULER
Decorative rulers help to create fast and easy page borders.

HOW TO USE TEMPLATES

- Press the template firmly against the paper with one hand. Use your other hand to trace inside or around the template shape with disappearing ink or a pencil. Lift the template and cut out the traced shape.

- Create page titles by matting template-traced and cut letters with colored paper so they visually pop off the page.

- Use templates to create perfect mats and borders.

Cathy Booth for Emagination Crafts

For fresh, innovative and inspiring punch art ideas, see Memory Makers Punch Your Art Out Volumes 1, 2 and 3 *(ordering information on page 126).*

PUNCHES

Punches are rugged little tools into which you insert a piece of paper, press on a button, and out pops a perfectly punched shape. Punches are available in hundreds of sizes, shapes and designs, including geometric patterns, letters and numbers. Some punches are designed to extend deep into the middle of a piece of paper, allowing you to punch shapes inches from your paper edge.

HOW TO USE PUNCHES

- To create perfect punched shapes, insert a piece of paper into the punch. Hold the paper firmly while pressing down on the button with your other hand. Carefully remove the paper and punched shape.

- Punch patterns into die cuts and then layer the die cuts over contrasting paper.

- Use the tiny punched shapes to decorate pages or mats.

- Place punched shapes close together to create page borders.

- Layer the punched shapes to "build"—make animals, vehicles, flowers and more.

- Combine punched shapes into "quilt" patterns for mats or borders.

- Use punched letters to create page titles.

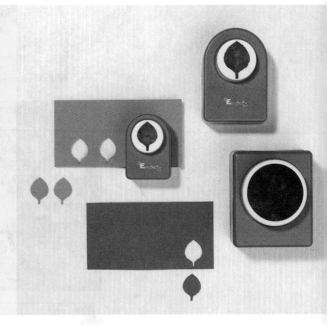

STICKERS

Stickers are one of the easiest ways to jazz up scrapbook pages. There are thousands to choose from in a multitude of colors, themes and styles—including letter and number, border, journaling and design element stickers. Stickers add such easy visual impact to a page that it is tempting to use them excessively, which can result in pages that appear disorganized or cluttered. Get the most impact from your stickers by using them selectively.

HOW TO USE STICKERS

• Draw a guideline for letter and border sticker placement. Use a template as a pattern, if needed.

• If stickers are misplaced, use adhesive remover to help lift them from the page.

• Large stickers can stand on their own, but smaller stickers have more impact when grouped together.

• Combine stickers with other page elements like photos or die cuts.

• Use stickers to frame photos by clustering them at the corners of the pictures or stringing them along the photo's sides.

• Accent titles with stickers.

• Use theme-related stickers to create "mini scenes."

• Use stickers to create page borders or to visually tie spreads together.

Andrea Grossman for Mrs. Grossman's Paper Company; Photos Mary Liz Curtin

STAMPS

How can something so simple create such gorgeous and impressive results? That's the beauty of rubber stamps. With just a few stamps and an inkpad, you can make delicate borders, lacy photo corners, stamped backgrounds, eye-catching photo mats, dressed-up die cuts and jazzy page accents. With the amazing array of stamp designs and inkpad colors available, it is easy to coordinate stamped images with any page design.

Pam Hornschu for Stampendous!® Inc.

HOW TO USE STAMPS

- Evenly apply ink to the rubber stamp pad. Tap the stamp against the pad to remove excess ink.

- Apply steady pressure (don't rock the stamp) when transferring the ink to your paper.

- Allow sufficient dry time. Dye pad ink dries quickly but pigment inks (preferable) take up to 24 hours. Shorten the drying time by holding stamped paper near a heat source for several minutes.

- Customize your stamped image by coloring within the border.

- Seal a stamped image with embossing powder, which raises the design, giving it additional dimension.

- Stamp mats, page borders, frames and titles.

- Add dimension to stamped images by cropping out tiny parts of the stamped image and adding colored paper to the back.

DIE CUTS

Die cuts are pre-cut paper shapes that come in both printed and solid colors. These decorative elements are great for adding theme accents to a page. Die cuts are sold individually and in packages. Increasing numbers of scrapbook and craft stores have centers where customers can cut their own die cuts for a small fee. Some shop owners may allow you to cut die cuts for free if you use paper purchased at their store. As with all paper and paper products, make sure your die cuts are acid- and lignin-free.

Sandi Genovese for Ellison Craft and Design
Photos Kevin Corcoran and Helen Jones

HOW TO USE DIE CUTS

- Apply adhesive to the back of your die cut and press firmly on your page. For self-adhesive die cuts, peel off the backing, and stick.

- Journal on the die cut.

- Use a die cut as a photo mat.

- Embellish die cuts with stickers or stamps. Add penned details.

- Use a punch to punch shapes into die cuts.

- Link several same-shaped die cuts together to form a paper chain border.

- Silhouette-crop photos of people and tuck them behind the windows of car-, bus-, and house-shaped die cuts.

Tool organization & care

Like most hobbies, scrapbooking involves a good number of tools and supplies. If you are like many scrapbookers, your stash of new products will seem to grow every time you turn around. Organization is the key to keeping your materials available and in good shape for scrapbooking ease. The following tips will help.

1 COLLECT YOUR SCRAPBOOK TOOLS AND SUPPLIES

Empty your storage areas, bins, drawers and other nooks and crannies, where you may have stuck scissors or conveniently stashed punches.

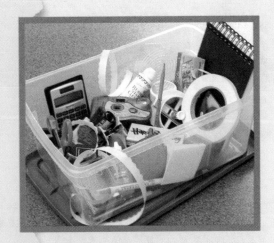

2 SORT YOUR TOOLS AND SUPPLIES

Sort items into piles such as "scissors", "pens", "stamps", "punches", "adhesives," etc. Set aside any damaged or unwanted items. Later you can give them away, host a swap night with scrapbooking friends or swap them on-line in one of the many chat groups devoted to scrapbooking. Sort paper by color. Separate scraps of paper from full sheets. Divide patterned paper, die cuts and stickers into piles defined either by color or by theme.

3 CLEAN AND LABEL YOUR TOOLS AND SUPPLIES

Before storing, replace cutter blades, clean tracing marks from templates, sharpen punches with aluminum foil, clean ink residue from stamps, test pens. Label tools with your name or initials to help identify them at crops. Create an inventory supplies checklist using the work sheet on page 45 while you have everything sorted. From that list, compile an ongoing shopping/wish list to avoid duplicate purchases, to share during gift-giving holidays or when you get that discount coupon from your local craft store.

4 STORE YOUR SUPPLIES

Protect your scrapbook investments by storing your freshly cleaned and organized tools and supplies in storage containers that will keep items dry, dust-free and easily accessible. Keep your supplies and workspace options in mind when shopping for storage containers. When storing supplies, the materials you use the most should be the easiest to access. Time spent on getting organized and money spent on storage containers will reward you with quick-and-easy scrapbooking!

HOW TO STORE AND CARE FOR YOUR TOOLS

• Store albums in an upright position. Allow sufficient room to avoid pressing tightly against other albums.

• Paper and paper supplies should be stored in a clean, dry place, out of direct sunlight. If possible, store paper horizontally.

• Pens must be tightly capped to prevent drying and stored away from heat. Some pigment pens are best stored on their side rather than upright.

• Adhesives should be stored out of the sun and away from direct heat.

• Stamps must be cleaned after each use with stamp cleaner solvent or warm, soapy water. Dry completely. Store in a dust-free environment.

• Punches must be stored in a dry, dust-free place to prevent rusting. Sharpen punches by punching through heavy aluminum foil or very fine grade sandpaper. Punch through wax paper to lubricate sticky punches.

• Cutter blades should be changed regularly when used often.

• Templates and rulers should be cleaned with warm, soapy water to remove ink, chalk residue and adhesive. Store templates inside three-ring binders.

• Store die cuts and stickers within page protectors inside of binders. CD jewel cases and videocassette cases make acceptable, inexpensive storage containers.

• Cutting mats should be cleaned, as needed, to remove adhesive residue.

Supplies checklist & wishlist

Keep in mind that you do not need everything listed here to get started; just start with the basics and build your supplies as your budget allows. Use one copy of this list to keep track of the supplies that you already have. Use a second copy of this checklist for a shopping list. Take both lists with you when shopping to avoid any unnecessary spending. Update both lists regularly to stay well-stocked and ready to crop while working toward your album goals.

ORGANIZATIONAL SUPPLIES
- [ ] *Photo box(es)*
- [ ] *Negative sleeves*
- [ ] *Photo envelopes*
- [ ] *Self-stick notes*
- [ ] *Memorabilia keepers*
- [ ] *Storage containers*

ALBUM TYPES
- [ ] *Strap*
- [ ] *Post bound*
- [ ] *Spiral*
- [ ] *3-ring binder*
- [ ] *Mini*
- [ ] *Other*

_____

Preferred brand(s)

_____
_____

ALBUM SIZES
- [ ] *4 x 6"*
- [ ] *5 x 7"*
- [ ] *8½ x 11"*
- [ ] *12 x 12"*
- [ ] *12 x 15"*
- [ ] *Other*

_____

Preferred brand(s)

_____
_____

ALBUM FILLER PAGES
- [ ] *4 x 6"*
- [ ] *5 x 7"*
- [ ] *8½ x 11"*
- [ ] *12 x 12"*
- [ ] *12 x 15"*
- [ ] *Other*

_____
_____

Preferred brand(s)

_____
_____

ALBUM PAGE PROTECTORS
- [ ] *4 x 6"*
- [ ] *5 x 7"*
- [ ] *8½ x 11"*
- [ ] *12 x 12"*
- [ ] *12 x 15"*

_____

Preferred brand(s)

_____
_____

ARCHIVAL QUALITY ADHESIVES
- [ ] *Photo splits*
- [ ] *Double-sided photo tape*
- [ ] *Tape roller*
- [ ] *Liquid glue pen*
- [ ] *Glue stick*
- [ ] *Bottled glue*
- [ ] *Self-adhesive foam spacers*
- [ ] *Adhesive application machine*
- [ ] *Adhesive application machine cartridge*
- [ ] *Adhesive remover*
- [ ] *Other*

_____
_____

Preferred brand(s)

_____
_____

SCISSORS & CUTTERS
- [ ] *Small scissors*
- [ ] *Regular scissors*
- [ ] *Decorative scissors*
- [ ] *Paper trimmer*
- [ ] *Shape cropper(s)*
- [ ] *Craft knife*

PENCILS, PENS, MARKERS
- [ ] *Pigment pen(s)*
- [ ] *Photo-safe pencil*
- [ ] *Vanishing ink pen*

RULERS & TEMPLATES
- [ ] *Metal straightedge ruler*
- [ ] *Grid ruler*
- [ ] *Decorative ruler(s)*
- [ ] *Journaling template(s)*
- [ ] *Shape template(s)*
- [ ] *Letter template(s)*
- [ ] *Nested template(s)*

ACID- AND LIGNIN-FREE PAPER
- [ ] *Red*
- [ ] *Orange*
- [ ] *Yellow*
- [ ] *Brown*
- [ ] *Green*
- [ ] *Blue*
- [ ] *Purple*
- [ ] *Pink*
- [ ] *Black*
- [ ] *White*
- [ ] *Patterns*

_____

- [ ] *Themes*

_____
_____

- [ ] *Vellum color(s)*

_____
_____

- [ ] *Mulberry color(s)*

_____
_____

- [ ] *Specialty paper(s)*

_____
_____

- [ ] *Other*

_____
_____

Preferred brand(s)

_____
_____

STICKERS
Themes or types

_____
_____
_____
_____
_____

DIE CUTS
Themes or types

_____
_____
_____
_____
_____
_____

PUNCHES
- [ ] *Corner rounder*
- [ ] *Hand punch(es)*
- [ ] *Border(s)*
- [ ] *Decorative corner(s)*
- [ ] *Photo mounting*
- [ ] *Shape(s)*

- [ ] *Tweezers*
- [ ] *Wax paper*
- [ ] *Aluminum foil*

RUBBER STAMPS
Themes or types

_____
_____
_____

- [ ] *Ink pad(s)*
- [ ] *Embossing powder(s)*
- [ ] *Stamp cleaner*

Our Wedding
June 25th 1989

With my parents
Connie Baron, Greg Baron
Our Wedding party

Organizing photos & memorabilia

As long as you continue to take pictures, you will continue to face the challenge of organizing your photos. Sorting and storing those shots and related memorabilia may seem intimidating. The key to success is finding a system that works for you. Take into consideration your personal accounting style. Are you the sort who updates and balances her checkbook regularly or are you more likely to toss receipts into a box and straighten out your accounts every few months? On the following pages, we'll show you two basic ways to organize your photos—chronologically and by theme. Both your personality and the scrapbook project may dictate which of these two options you can best employ.

While the process of sorting and storing your photos may seem overwhelming at first, I promise that the effort will make future scrapbooking projects easier and more enjoyable. As with most challenging endeavors, the first step is often the most difficult. I encourage you to dive in and get started.

Sorting a lifetime of photos

All serious scrapbookers eventually have to face "the drawer," where throughout the years photos have been tossed and tossed and tossed. There they reside, in a hodge-podge jumble, waiting for you to have the time and the courage to organize them. With a bit of direction and the work sheet provided (see page 45), you will find the task easier than you might think. This process works great for sorting a lifetime of photos chronologically. If you are interested in doing theme albums, you can always pull the theme photos out later and they'll already be in chronological order!

A Decade of Memories

It took a week and a whole room to start the sorting process.

These sheets are what made the whole process even possible.

WHAT YOU WILL NEED:

- Archival-quality photo boxes
- Photo-safe envelopes
- Archival-quality box for memorabilia
- Journaling pen
- Blank sticky notes
- Work sheet from page 45

Michele stayed true to her belief that "you just have to take a deep breath and go!" when she recently organized ten years of photos.

1 Start by photocopying the work sheet on page 45. Make a separate copy for each year or decade of photos represented. Date each form with an appropriate year or decade. Then focus your attention on one work sheet at a time.

2 Notice that the work sheet is divided into boxes which are labeled with the months of the year. If working with decades, cross out the "month" and insert "years". Within each box write down major events that occurred within that time period. Include such things as family birthdays (and the ages they achieved), when children began the school year (and the name of the school and grade attended), and when and where you vacationed. Use old journals, calendars and date books to supplement your information.

3 As you complete one work sheet, move on to the next. Spread out finished work sheets on a large surface. Begin matching photos to the events noted on the work sheets. Continue until all photos have been sorted. Store the newly created groupings in photo-safe envelopes inside archival-quality boxes until you are ready to scrapbook.

I'm getting closer!

A lot of detective work went into getting pictures in the right year. Ahh! feels so good to be finished!

It took Michele and a scrapbooking friend a week to organize more than a thousand photos. After being sorted, the pictures were stored in photo-safe envelopes, within archival-quality boxes. Now that her photos are organized, Michele finds it much easier to move forward with her scrapbooking projects. "It was an enormous job, and I could never have done it without my friend's help," Michele recalls. "But in the end, the work was definitely worth it!"

Work sheet to sort photos

YEAR: _____

JANUARY	**JULY**
FEBRUARY	**AUGUST**
MARCH	**SEPTEMBER**
APRIL	**OCTOBER**
MAY	**NOVEMBER**
JUNE	**DECEMBER**

Source: Barbara Tolopilo, Family Treasures, Inc.

Sorting photos chronologically

Like many scrapbookers, you may find it easiest to begin organizing your most recent photos and memorabilia first. Those are the pictures and stories about which you will remember the most. Find a space out of direct sunlight where photos may be left spread out for a long period of time if needed. Follow these four simple steps for sorting photos from the current year in chronological order.

WHAT YOU WILL NEED:

- 1 or 2 archival-quality photo boxes
- Photo-safe envelopes
- Archival-quality box for memorabilia
- Journaling pen
- Blank sticky notes

PLAYING DETECTIVE

Identifying and dating unlabeled photos requires a bit of sleuthing. If friends or family can't help, study the photos for clues.

- Fashions change frequently and provide strong clues for dating photos. Pick up a book on fashion trends at your library or bookstore for help.

- Hairstyles change as often as fashions. Ask a local hairdresser about the styles.

- Children's looks change radically from year to year. When trying to date a photo, study the children in the images. Their height, weight, and the number of teeth they have will speak volumes.

- Makes and models of cars change over time. The appearance of the automobiles in photos can narrow down the year.

- Signs and billboards may offer clues as to when and where the pictures were taken.

- The location where the photo was shot—whether a neighborhood or vacation spot—can offer important clues.

1 *Gather all your photos and memorabilia from the current year. If the photos are still in their original envelopes with the negatives, transfer them to photo-safe envelopes. We'll deal with storing negatives later in this chapter.*

2 *Label the contents of each photo envelope, or label the dividers in the photo-safe boxes. Include a "best guess" date as to when the pictures were taken. If there is related memorabilia, note it with a star next to the date. Jot down and store with the photos any information you may want to include when journaling.*

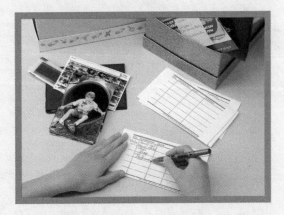

3 *Sort the envelopes by date. Assign each envelope a number which will assist you in filing them in consecutive order. Place them in the box.*

4 *Sort your memorabilia by category such as "tickets," "journals," or "brochures." Place the items in a labeled and dated memorabilia box. If you have kept an annual journal or calendar, this is a good place to store it.*

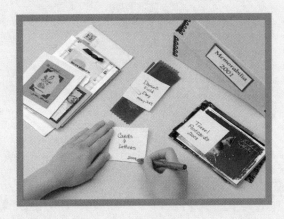

Sorting photos by theme

Sorting photos and memorabilia by theme works particularly well if you are planning wedding, anniversary or vacation albums. You may also wish to use this method for creating scrapbooks featuring family events such as daily life, school days, celebrations, holidays, etc. We will examine theme albums in more detail later. But for now, follow the steps given to organize your photos by theme.

WHAT YOU WILL NEED:

- 1 or 2 archival-quality photo boxes
- Photo-safe envelopes
- Archival-quality box for memorabilia
- Journaling pen
- Blank sticky notes

MAKING JOURNALING NOTES

Journaling is an important part of preserving memories. Keep a pad of paper nearby when sorting and cataloging your photos and memorabilia. As you organize your pictures, take time to jot down any information that comes to mind. Include details such as the names of those in the images, the date the photos were taken, the location of the events and any thoughts or feelings you may have related to the pictures.

1 Collect your photos and memorabilia. On sticky notes, write down the categories pertinent to your current project. If, for example, you are working on a wedding album, you may wish to sort the photos into groups such as Getting Ready, Ceremony, Portraits, Reception, and Honeymoon. Categories for a holiday album might include Easter, Fourth of July, or Christmas. Spread the labeled sticky notes on a large work surface that is out of direct sunlight.

2 Sort your photos by category into piles near the appropriate sticky notes.

3 Re-sort the photos in each pile so they fall in logical order. This is, most often, the sequence in which you hope to place the photos in your album. Place the sorted piles in labeled, photo-safe envelopes and acid-free boxes, storing them until you are ready to scrapbook.

Storing photos & negatives

While the look of a storage container doesn't matter, making sure you've got the right container and are storing your keepsakes in the correct environment will save your photos and negatives from damage. There are numerous photo-safe storage containers available. When selecting one, make sure it is the right size to house your pictures, and the right shape to store on your shelves.

STORING PHOTOS

Store photos in photo-safe envelopes and containers in a dark, dry place or within page protectors in a scrapbook album. While some cardboard boxes are acid-free, most are not. And since most cardboard boxes are prone to collapse and won't protect photos from environmental hazards, use them only for temporary storage. If buying a plastic storage system, choose one made of either acrylic, polypropylene, polyethylene or polyester. Store at temperatures between 65-70 degrees and with 30-50 percent humidity.

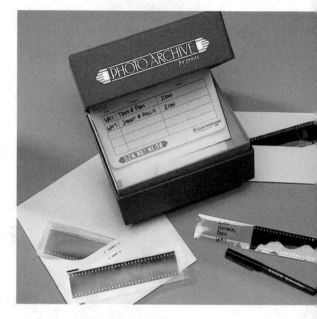

A well-organized negative storage system not only protects a critical backup but also makes it easy to order reprints and enlargements. When using an envelope system, place individual negatives in paper or plastic sleeves. Then insert your sleeved negatives in labeled archival envelopes organized in an acid-free, lignin-free box. For backup, store your photos and negatives in separate places. If disaster strikes, one or the other is likely to survive.

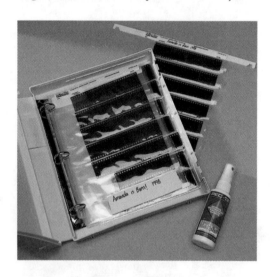

STORING NEGATIVES

Before storing dirty negatives, clean them with a commercial negative cleaner. Store negatives in negative sleeves, storage binders or storage boxes. The storage vehicles should be 100 percent acid-, lignin-, and PVC-free. If storing negatives in acid-free envelopes, separate strips with acid-free paper to prevent sticking. Keep negatives away from dust, bright light, excessive heat, and high humidity. Store at temperatures between 65-70 degrees and with 30-50 percent humidity.

HOW TO SCAN PHOTOS

A scanner takes a photo and translates the image into a digital format that can be read by, stored in, displayed on and printed from a computer. The scanner breaks an image into units of measure called "pixels" (picture elements) or "dpi" (dots per inch). To scan a standard photo at home, use the best possible original. When scanning and printing an image for a scrapbook page, use a resolution of 150-300 dpi (72 dpi for Web site images). Scale the photo to the desired size, select the type of image (grayscale for black-and-white; millions of colors for color photos), and save as a TIFF file for long-term computer storage (or JPEG if you intend to e-mail the photo or place it on a Web site). The quality of your printed photo depends on the quality of your scanner, scanning software, printer and the paper on which you print.

If do-it-yourself scanning is not for you, get high-quality photo scans put on a CD at a camera store, mini lab or professional lab. To print images from a CD, a high-quality color printer and photo-quality printer paper will give the best color results.

Photos Orealys Hernandez
Holly Springs, North Carolina

DIGITAL PHOTO STORAGE

Increasing numbers of today's scrapbookers are storing their regular and digital photos on CDs. Unlike negatives, the images saved to CDs do not wear out; with proper care they can last 100 years or more! Sealed in plastic and metal, they are more immune to everyday mishaps such as scratches, spills and accidental bending. Experts recommend storing photo CDs individually in acrylic jewel cases, not in soft plastic sleeves which may adhere to the disc upon exposure to heat and humidity.

Store jewel cases in a closed box, drawer or cabinet to protect them from sunlight, dust and climate changes. Storage temperatures should be between 50-77 degrees with 20-50 percent relative humidity. CDs should also be protected from sharp objects such as pens and pencils, solvents and fingerprints. If needed, clean discs with a lens tissue, gently wiping from the center of the disc in a radial direction toward the outside edge of the disc. Some manufacturers also produce lens cleaner that is safe to use on CDs, but it is wise to check with the product manufacturer before applying any chemicals.

Photos Becky Baanhofman
Littleton, Colorado

White Fence Farm

April 2001

Lakewood, Colorado

Sasha age 8

Anna age 11

Celebrating Easter and sneaking in some family photos.

Making your first page

It is time to take a breath and make the leap, time to start working on your first scrapbook page! Sometimes that blank scrapbook page can be a little intimidating. Put away any preconceptions you may have about how your page should look. Remember that there is no "right" or "wrong" way when it comes to creating pages. Each spread is a unique reflection of its creator. As you grow as a scrapbooker, you will define your own personal style. Your pages will go through a style evolution as you master new scrapbook techniques.

In this chapter, we will introduce you to design basics, different methods of photo cropping, how to create a pleasing photo mat, mounting photos and much more. We encourage you to draw inspiration from these pages and from the pages of those around you. Pick up a magazine or book about scrapbooking for more ideas. Enjoy experimenting. Enjoy telling your story.

> FIRST-TIME JITTERS ARE PART OF THE LEARNING PROCESS, BUT TRY TO SET THEM ASIDE WHEN YOU REACH FOR YOUR WONDERFUL NEW SUPPLIES.
>
> *–Michele*

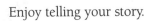

An overview of the page-making process

Making pages is easier when you break down and order the process. Take your time and enjoy each step of the way. In scrapbooking, as in many things, the journey is just as important as the destination. Here is a simple overview of the page-making process. We will examine it in more detail on the following pages.

❶ SELECT PHOTOS
Photos are one of the most important elements on your scrapbook pages. Spend time selecting the perfect shots for each spread. Consider the mood and intent of the page. Find pictures that carry your message.

❷ SELECT PAPER COLORS
Color selection can make the difference between a great and not-so-great scrapbook page. The paper colors that you choose to help showcase your photos will affect the way you and others feel when looking at the finished album. Pick colors that convey the right emotion and complement your photos.

❸ LAYOUT AND DESIGN
Before adhering anything to a page, take the time to move your photos around. Experiment with different positions. Try overlapping pictures. Drag some to the page edge. Tip them. Turn them. Find a placement that looks balanced and draws focus to your best shots.

4 CROP PHOTOS

Cropping, or cutting photos, enhances the image and eliminates unwanted portions of the shot. Through cropping, you can focus the viewer's eye on a particular element of the picture and remove extraneous portions that detract from its impact.

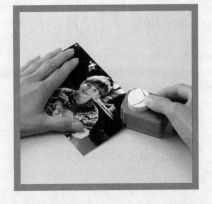

5 MAT PHOTOS

A mat goes beneath the photo and helps visually "pop" the picture off the page. Mats can also help protect photos by forming a barrier between them and unsafe embellishments or memorabilia.

6 MOUNT PAGE ELEMENTS

Mounting is the process of attaching matted photos and memorabilia on your scrapbook album pages with photo-safe adhesives. Some nonpermanent mounting techniques allow easy removal of photos and documents for copying or restoration.

7 ADD TITLE, JOURNALING AND ACCESSORIES

Page titles and journaling are the voices that bring your photos to life. They record information that may seem obvious at the present, but can be lost over time. A title should capture the essence of the page. Journal the facts, such as when and where the photo was taken. Accessorize the page with punch art, stickers and die cuts. Do so sparingly to keep the focus on the photos and their stories.

Select photos

Scrapbookers love their photos and many are determined to find room on their pages for every single picture. This is not always a good idea. Overcrowded pages do a disservice to the truly wonderful shots. In order to create good pages you must cull photos. Begin by spreading your pictures on a table and examining them. Choose the photos that truly speak to you and are of highest quality. The 3-5 pictures you select to feature on each album page should work well together, complementing each other's colors, composition and content.

To select photos, spread them all out on a table and examine them. Which photos really speak to you? Which do you notice first? Are they high quality? Do they have good color? Are they in focus? These are the photos you scrapbook.

WHAT TO DO WITH EXTRA PHOTOS

You can always save and store extra photos to use in future albums. Or put those extra pictures to use right now!

- Cut the faces from extra pictures to use as page decorations. Tuck them in the middle of a flower die cut, on an Easter egg or on a Christmas decoration.

- Use them in "star pupil" displays for your child's special day at school.

- Incorporate extra pictures in other craft projects such as when you're making greeting cards, calendars, gift tags and collages.

- Punch shapes from the photos, cut letters for page titles and other embellishments to use on your scrapbook pages.

- Give your children photos to practice their own cutting and cropping skills.

- Trade extra photos with family members who may have photos you've been coveting.

GETTING PHOTOS FROM RELATIVES

Most scrapbookers find it distressing when a particular family photo seems beyond reach. But with tenderness and tenacity there are often ways to include those treasures in your books. Many relatives are more likely to share their pictures when they better understand why you need them and exactly what you plan to do with them. Sharing this information, as well as your excitement, may inspire them to give you the pictures you desire. Promise not to use any pictures they may deem embarrassing, and to credit the photo's owner for each picture you do include. If the owner of the pictures is afraid to release them for fear they may be damaged or lost, invite her to accompany you to have the photos copied. If she lives a distance away, pay for all reproduction fees and shipping costs. Above all, promise to treat the photos with respect and care. Copy the pages on which you feature the borrowed pictures and present your relative with an album of her own as a thank-you gift.

HOW TO TAKE BETTER PHOTOS

- Keep a camera nearby to capture that unexpected but to-die-for shot.

- Use the right speed of film.

- Get close in order to better see your subject and eliminate extraneous backgrounds.

- Keep the background simple.

- Frame the subject off-center.

- Include some foreground to help put the picture in perspective.

- Watch your lighting. Bright overhead light creates unattractive shadows and is unflattering to your subject.

- Hold steady. Movement can blur pictures.

Photo Mary Jo Regier, Littleton, Colorado

Select paper colors

Color affects our thoughts and emotions as well as our physiology. Looking at certain colors increases or decreases the heart rate and blood pressure. Some colors (red) inspire energetic feelings while others (green) are calming. When selecting colors for your scrapbook pages, choose shades that are consistent with the mood of the spread.

Draw colors from your photos. You may wish to pick up on the blue in the background sky, or the green of grass, the color of an outfit or the hue of a person's eyes. Once having determined a primary color, choose other colors that complement your primary choice.

If you aren't confident about choosing colors, consider buying papers in presorted packages. These packets come with corresponding, coordinating papers in color and theme variations. Prepackaged papers help take the guesswork out of paper selection.

Can't figure out what colors to use? Pick up a color wheel at your local art or craft store. A color wheel has a rotating dial that helps users choose colors that work together harmoniously. The wheel shows complementary colors (colors that fall directly opposite each other on the wheel, such as green and red), and other combinations. There are dozens of ways to use the color wheel when scrapbooking.

HOW PAPER COLOR SETS A MOOD

Color helps sets a mood on both these scrapbook pages. The cool blues and greens used on the page to the right reflect and convey the peaceful calm of a child's lazy afternoon swing. The page below captures the glow of a southwest sunset by playing on the glowing orange shades in the sun-drenched rock formations in the background.

Ron Gerbrandt, Denver, Colorado
Photo Tonya Jeppson, Boise, Idaho

Photo Jeff Derksen, Denver, Colorado

HOW PAPER COLOR SHOWS CONTRAST

In the example below, the background color swallows up the photos. Generally, photos with a light background will get lost on a light-colored background page. Note how these same photos "pop" off the page when a darker background is used.

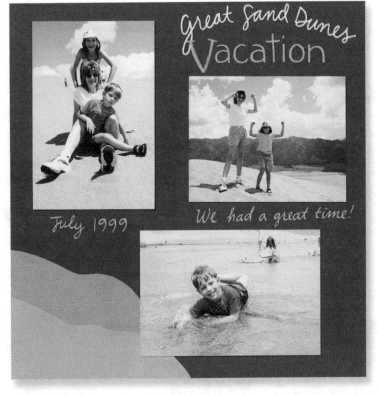

Layout and design

A good scrapbook page draws in the viewer. It is a comfortable place, an interesting place for her to rest her eyes. While the quality of the photos and color choices affect the success of the page, equally important to its impact is its layout and design.

A well-designed page has a strong focal point. This may be a photo, title or other element that draws the eye. Good pages also have a sense of balance. A substantial photo in one corner, for example, can be balanced by a heavy photo in its opposite corner. On the other hand, the scrapbooker may use several smaller elements grouped together to balance the visually heavier piece. Some artists ensure symmetry on a spread by mirroring the layout on the left page with the one on the right. On page 63, we have provided a few samples of simple layouts that work well.

When designing your page, make sure design elements support, rather than compete with, the photos, journaling and memorabilia. Use them sparingly and remember that white space is an important part of good design.

Move your photos around on the background pages, arranging and rearranging until you have a visually appealing layout that looks balanced.

BEFORE AND AFTER SCRAPBOOK PAGES

Simply by rearranging the same five photo elements and journaling, the scrapbook artist has turned a badly-designed page into one that is pleasing to the eye.

POOR LAYOUT AND DESIGN

- The top of the page is photo-heavy, unbalancing the layout.

- Layered photos seem to have been placed at random.

- The top edges of the layered photos create a senseless, jagged stair step.

- The silhouetted photo is "floating" and needs to be anchored.

- The photo in the top right corner is too close to the border.

- Photos seem to be grouped arbitrarily.

- Photos are tilted in different directions.

- White space is unevenly distributed.

- Journaling is clumped and difficult to read.

- The title doesn't pop.

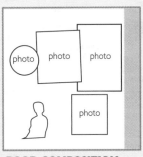

POOR COMPOSITION

Celebrating Easter and sneaking in some family photos.

Daniel age 6

Sasha age 8

Anna age 11

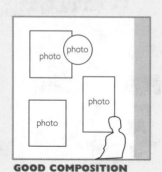

GOOD COMPOSITION

photo photo

photo

photo

GOOD LAYOUT AND DESIGN

- The top and bottom of the page are now equally weighted.

- Photos featuring the same subject have been grouped together.

- The silhouetted photo is anchored to the bottom of the page.

- Journaling is spread out, making it easier to read.

- White space is evenly distributed.

- The page title is prominent.

Scrapbook page design work sheet

It is simple to create well-balanced page layouts. Below are just a few samples of quick-and-easy page designs to get you started. As you become more involved in the hobby, you may find page designs that you really like in scrapbooking magazines or idea books. We've left some blank pages on this work sheet so that you can sketch your own quick-and-easy page designs for future reference.

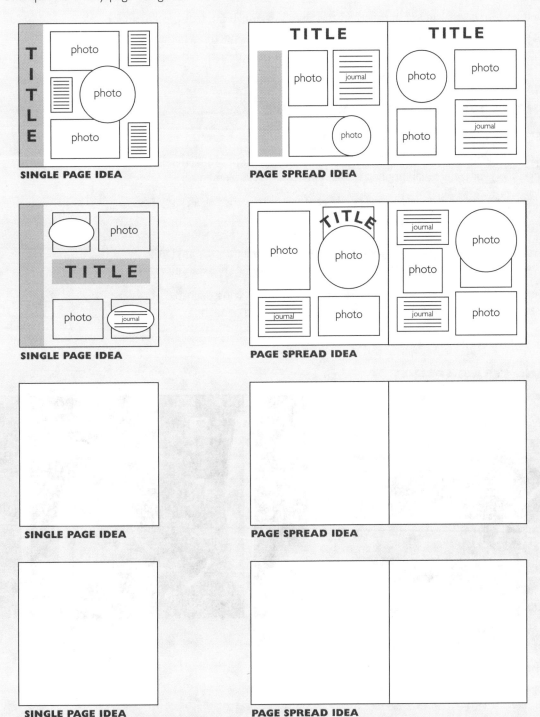

Crop photos

People often boil down the act and art of scrapbooking to one word "crop." Those who work on scrapbooks are "croppers." When they are "cropping" in groups it is called a "crop." To crop means to trim a photo in order to enhance it, or draw attention to the main subject.

Cutting pictures into hearts, circles, stars and other shapes is so much fun that people can forget the big picture. While cropping isn't the sole focus of scrapbooking, the more you know about when, why and how to crop, the better prepared you'll be to design your pages.

WHEN TO CROP AND WHEN NOT TO CROP

- Crop in order to add style and variety to your page.

- Crop to eliminate unwanted portions of the picture including photo blemishes, strangers in your pictures, lab printing errors and out-of-focus elements.

- Crop to draw emphasis to important portions of the picture such as a child's face.

- Crop to create a new piece of art.

- You may crop Polaroid peel-apart photos because the final print is separated from the reactive chemicals. Other Polaroid products may release harmful chemicals if cropped.

- Never crop original, historical or one-of-a-kind photos; you will lose valuable background information. Have reprints made if you wish to crop them.

CROPPING STRAIGHT LINES

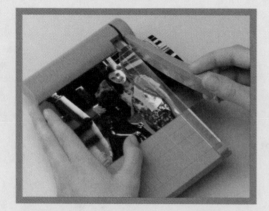

Straight cropping can be done with a personal paper trimmer (see page 31). Paper trimmers ensure perfectly straight cuts and are great for making 90 degree angles. When you feel more comfortable with cropping photos, try using a craft knife and a metal straightedge ruler. Hold the photo and ruler down tightly to avoid slippage.

CROPPING CORNERS

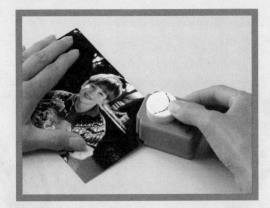

Corner cropping softens the look of a photo by removing small amounts from the photo's corners. Corner rounder punches are the perfect tool to accomplish this effect. Simply slide the punch onto the photo's corner and firmly push down on the button. Repeat on all four corners.

CROPPING WITH DECORATIVE SCISSORS

1 Before cutting with your decorative scissors, use a wax pencil and metal straightedge ruler to create guidelines for your incision.

2 Use decorative scissors to cut just a bit to the outside of the cutting line. Wipe remaining pencil marks away with a dry, soft cloth.

CROPPING SHAPES

While standard square and rectangular photos suit many scrapbook spreads, there are times when a page just screams for a photo of a different shape. Use a template or shape cutter to crop your pictures into circles, hearts, animals or other shapes.

❶ *Place the template over your photo and trace with a wax pencil, or for mark-free cropping, trace the shape with an embossing stylus or knitting needle.*

❷ *Cut out the shape, staying inside the line so markings will not show on your final image or wipe remaining pencil marks away with a soft, dry cloth.*

CROPPING SILHOUETTES

Silhouette cropping entails trimming around the contours of the subject in your photos. Silhouetting allows you to remove unnecessary backgrounds and direct visual focus to the important portions of a picture. With less extraneous image, you can also use more photos on a scrapbook page. Use small, sharp scissors to silhouette crop around people in photos. Cut slowly, following each person's outline. Be especially careful when cutting around hair and facial features.

CROPPING PARTIAL SILHOUETTES

When silhouette cropping, pick and choose the portions of the photo you wish to remove. There may be times when you would like to leave the sides or lower edge of a picture intact and remove just the upper portion of the photo. What and how much of the photo is cut away is totally up to you. Use a sharp craft knife to crop around the tiny parts of each photo that are not accessible with small scissors.

Mat photos

Matting is one of the easiest ways to emphasize a photo. One creatively matted photo can become the focal point on a page, or several matted photos can tie together different page elements. Mats add color and contrast to monotone photos that might otherwise disappear into the background. Matting helps establish the color theme for a page and should work well with other paper and decorative elements. Freehand cut, or use a template or shape cutter, to create a mat. Accent mats with stickers, punched shapes or stamped images.

Use a template or shape cutter to create a mat for your cropped photo by cutting the mat ⅛" or larger than your photo. You can also freehand cut a mat. Here are more simple ideas for creating photo mats.

Cut two mats the same size, center the photo on one and mount the second mat askew.

For a perfectly shaped mat for photos that are silhouetted or partially silhouetted, use a Magic Matter™ to trace around the photo on paper of choice. Then cut out the mat.

Trim the edges of photos and mats
with decorative scissors and punches.

Use a corner slot punch (or photo mounting
punch) to create a mat into which you slip the
corners of your photo.

Use mats for journaling by writing directly
on the mat around the photo.

Vary the shape of photos and mats.
You may wish, for example, to place
a round photo on a square mat, or
do just the opposite.

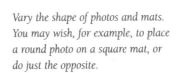

Experiment with double- and triple-matting photos
in different colored papers.

Mount page elements

Mounting photos or memorabilia is the process of attaching them to an album page. You may choose to put them in your album in a way that ensures they will be a part of the page permanently. Or, you may wish to place them in the album so that they can be removed at a later date.

PERMANENT MOUNTING

Permanent mounting requires the application of adhesive to the back of a photo or mat. Photo splits and tape rollers do the job neatly. Avoid liquid glues that may buckle the photo. Apply adhesive to all four corners of your image and again in the center. You may wish to add additional adhesive to ensure bonding.

NONPERMANENT MOUNTING

Nonpermanent mounting allows you to attach your items to a page and still have the option of easily moving them. This method is especially beneficial when placing materials in your scrapbook that you may wish to have duplicated someday. The easiest way to temporarily mount items is to use self-adhesive photo corners. These paper or plastic triangular pockets are applied to the album page. The photo's corners are then inserted into each pocket.

Add title, journaling & accessories

The last step to completing your scrapbook page is adding a title, journaling, and any embellishments you have selected. You'll find more about journaling and titles in the last chapter. Remember, any decorative touches you add to your finished page should support, rather than detract, from your photos.

TITLE

A title, whether created freehand, with stickers, punched or stamped shapes, or computer-generated fonts, sums up the page's content and theme. It gives readers a "heads-up" so they can be better prepared for the material to come.

JOURNALING

A picture may speak a thousand words, but words do something photos cannot. They record important information such as the names of those in photos as well as when, where and why the picture was shot. They are the vehicle for sharing insights and stories that make pages unique. That's why good journaling is an important part of good scrapbook pages.

Reluctant journalers often fear their handwriting is not attractive, their spelling is bad or they cannot express themselves succinctly. If you share these concerns, try writing on separate pieces of paper, cutting them out and applying them to your pages rather than writing directly on the page. Or use a computer to help write and check your spelling. However you journal, let your personality flow with the ink and your pages will come alive.

ACCESSORIES

Adhere design elements—borders, stickers, punch art, die cuts and stamped images— to finish the page, remembering that sometimes "less is more."

The complete page

A successful scrapbook page tells a story with photos, memorabilia and journaling. It is well-balanced and pleasing to look at.
The colors help convey the mood and message of the page.
Accents add that special zing. A successful scrapbook page is
more than just a display of photos. It is a work of art.

Donna Leicht, Appleton, Wisconsin

Lisa Jackson, San Antonio, Texas

Joyce Schweitzer, Greensboro, North Carolina

Karen Regep Glover, Grosse Pointe Woods, Michigan

LauraLinda Rudy, Markham
ON, Canada

Creating page continuity

Two is often better than one, especially with scrapbook pages. Sometimes you just have too many great photos to fit on just one page. For page continuity, the key is to unify two pages to read as one, so your story can flow from page to page harmoniously. Here are some ideas to help you make your double-page spreads come together.

USE A BORDER Visually connect a double-page spread by using a border that runs across both pages. The border can extend around all four sides of the layout or simply run across the upper and lower edges.

Sandi Parrish, Grand Rapids, Michigan

USE THE SAME BACK-GROUND PAPER This is the easiest way to keep your eyes flowing across both pages and eliminate the perception of delineation.

Cindy Mandernach, Grand Blanc, Michigan

COORDINATE COLORS Coordinate your page décor for an ensemble look. Use different, yet matching, paper for your second page to pull the look together.

CREATE MOVEMENT Pop-ups, peek-a-boos and moving parts can extend across two pages and add interest.

SPLIT PHOTOS OR DESIGN ELEMENTS
Consider cutting photos in half and placing each section on either side of the gutter close to the seam. This works especially well with panoramic scenery shots and photo enlargements.

MIRROR A DESIGN
Repeat the same layout on both sides of the spread, or create a reverse mirror by flipping the layout upside down on the opposite page. Keep shapes and matting identical.

RUN A TITLE ACROSS THE SPREAD
Running a title across the spread draws the viewer's eye from one side to the next. Titles can also be butted up against the gutter seam, diagonally across the spread or on the side borders of both pages.

ALLOW CONTACT
When photos touch, your eyes follow them along the sequence. Allow the pictures to flow across the gutter of two pages.

REPEAT A DESIGN ELEMENT
Place similar embellishments on both pages such as punch art, stickers, die cuts or stamps.

ZOO CREW

OUR VISIT TO CHEYENNE MOUNTAIN ZOO IN COLORADO SPRINGS DURING SPRING BREAK MARCH 2001. THIS WAS THE FIRST TIME WE VISITED THIS ZOO.

SASHA'S FAVORITES WERE THE WOLVES. DANIEL'S FAVORITES WERE THE LIONS AND VULTURES. ANNA'S FAVORITES WAS THE GORILLAS.
ANNA 11 DANIEL 6
SASHA 8

Making your first album

Congratulations! You have finished that first page! Now it's time to focus on the bigger picture—the creation of an album. Some believe that an album is simply a collection of individual pages, but it is much more. A successful album is cohesive and organized. When possible, the design flows from spread to spread. A good album is a substantial package that is both beautiful and informative.

Just as there are two basic methods for organizing photos and memorabilia, there are two basic types of scrapbooks. The first type displays the photos in chronological order so the pictures follow a time line. The second type of scrapbook is a theme album in which the scrapbooker pulls together and displays photos and memorabilia surrounding a particular topic or theme. Many scrapbookers keep both chronological and theme albums. Once you begin thinking of the number of ways you can present your photos, you'll find your ideas multiplying and your creative dreams becoming reality.

IF YOU'RE LIKE ME, YOU WILL WANT TO DO 'THIS' TYPE OF ALBUM AND THEN 'THAT' TYPE OF ALBUM ALL AT THE SAME TIME—AND THEN FIT ANOTHER ONE IN BETWEEN. I SAY GO FOR IT! THERE'S NO REASON TO LIMIT YOURSELF.

—Michele

Chronological albums

In a chronological or on going album, a scrapbooker organizes the photos sequentially, displaying the pictures in the order in which events happened. Some scrapbookers choose to dedicate one album to each month or calendar year. Others may create an album for each child or family member and then order the pages within that book chronologically. A chronological album is a wonderful way to ensure that future generations will have a true grasp on how and when events unfolded.

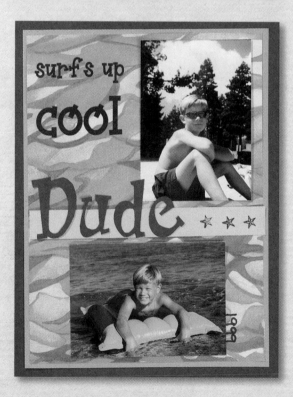

Oksanna Pope, of Los Gatos California, is making a chronological, on going album that cleverly does two things: it preserves special memories for her son and it documents Royce's annual milestones of age progression.

With her use of close-up, single subject photos and very simple page designs and embellishments, Oksanna is able to keep the focus of her album on one thing—her son!

Kelly Angard, of Highlands Ranch, Colorado, is typical
of many scrapbookers in that she faithfully keeps up
with her scrapbooking as she gets photos back from the
photo lab. In doing so, she has a consistent chronology
of her family's life, including day-to-day events as well
as special occasions and celebrations.

The hallmark of great chronological-order albums is the documentation of dates and the ages of those shown in the photos. By providing these details through journaling, viewers get a good glimpse of a family's progression over the course of time.

Theme albums

A theme album is limited to a single topic and may feature activities in which you are involved repeatedly over the course of years. It may also focus on a single event such as a wedding, vacation or hobby. Good theme albums owe their success to the consistent use of paper colors, patterns, journaling and decorative elements. On page 87 you will find a work sheet on which to note ideas for future theme album projects. Once you finish a theme album you'll undoubtedly look forward to beginning another.

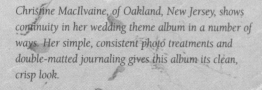

Christine MacIlvaine, of Oakland, New Jersey, shows continuity in her wedding theme album in a number of ways. Her simple, consistent photo treatments and double-matted journaling gives this album its clean, crisp look.

Doris Lemert, Fort Wayne, Indiana

ABC ALBUM ABC albums are a fun alternative to a chronologically ordered theme album, and you can make an ABC album for just about any theme! Each page or layout features photos, memorabilia and page accents that relate to a certain letter of the alphabet. Enhance an ABC album by journaling with words that start with each letter of the alphabet and that apply to the album's theme or its photos.

BABY ALBUM A baby album is a record of the milestones of pregnancy, the wonder of birth and those awesome "firsts"—from a child's first smile to the first toddling steps. The album can include photos, sonograms, notes from birth preparation classes, hospital brochures, birth announcements, congratulatory cards, scraps of wrapping paper and clips of downy hair from a child's first haircut.

HOBBY ALBUM Whether your passion is piano or soccer, building model cars or racing dune buggies, you'll want to record your pleasure and progress in a hobby album. Have someone take pictures of you participating in your favorite activity. If you are creating something, whether in clay, stone, fabric or another medium, take step-by-step photos that show the progress of your work. Purchase or buy pockets in which to store small awards or objects such as coins, flat seashells and collectible cards. Or photocopy these items as well as embroidery or other stitched works for inclusion in the album.

Terri Robichon
Plymouth, Minnesota

NEW HOME Remember the excitement of moving into a new home with photos of the construction, loading and unloading of the van, picture hanging afternoons, the unpacking of boxes, copies of mortgage papers and floor plans, journaled first impressions of neighbors, paint chips and wallpaper and fabric samples. Long after you've settled in and your house becomes a home, you'll look back through this album with triumph.

Melanie Duffy, Costa Mesa, California

PET ALBUM Pets add so much to our lives and ask for so little in return. Capture the essence of your pets and the loving relationship you share by preserving photos of daily antics and portraits, memorial tributes and labels from favorite food products. Don't forget to preserve locks of fur, feathers and I.D. tags in memorabilia keepers. Add photocopies of registered documents and certificates, too.

SEASON ALBUM The nip of fall air, the woody smell of winter, the colors of spring and the sounds of summer all evoke memories of special activities and events related to the changing seasons. Capture the moments in a seasonal album filled with photos, keepsakes, poems and journaling as you mark the passage of time.

*Kristi Hazelrigg
Washington, Oklahoma*

The buildings in Downtown Denver were just amazing. The picture above captures the Hyatt Regency track in the reflection of a neighboring high rise. We enjoyed the skyline throughout the day, but it was spectacular in the early morning sun and at sunset.

Joellyn Borke-Johnston
Des Moines, Iowa

JUNE 7, 1999   DAY 2.

KEARNEY, NE. → DENVER, CO

Fortunately, Mark had provided us with a map and we navigated well. Upon inquiry and confirmation, Karrah then declared the Hyatt Regency to be a 1st Class Hotel. Although, the origin of her question is unknown, it seems clear she defined a difference between this and our Super 8 lodging experiences!

The drive today into Denver was an exhilarating one for Mom and the kids. From the barest siting of the mountains on the horizon to realizing their majesty up close. Our approach was very exciting for all of us. Once we found ourselves in Denver proper, Mom was concerned with the difficulty that we might encounter finding our hotel, the Hyatt Regency.

TRAVEL ALBUM Whether you find adventure around the block or around the world, it's worth recording. Travel albums capture the excitement of those trips to the local park, to Granny's house in Texas, or to museums throughout Europe. Include special souvenirs and memorabilia such as maps, brochures, receipts, ticket stubs, train and plane tickets, itineraries, menus and pressed flowers—anything you collect on your journey.

Album goals work sheet

As you organize your photos and memorabilia, you are likely to come across specific albums you would like to create for yourself or for others. Use this work sheet to help you determine and define the albums you may wish to create over the course of time.

ALBUM TYPE (spiral, strap, mini, etc.)	ALBUM THEME	ALBUM FOR?	PHOTOS & MEMORABILIA ORGANIZED?	PRODUCTS TO PURCHASE	DATE STARTED	FINISH ALBUM BY?	NOTES
	Baby						
	Child						
	Family						
	Friendship						
	Heritage						
	Hobby or Career						
	Holiday						
	Portrait						
	School Days						
	The Seasons						
	Traditions						
	Travel						
	Tribute						
	Wedding						

An overview of the album-making process

The idea of creating an entire album can seem overwhelming. But with organization and planning,

your album can easily take shape. Don't hurry the process. Remember, this is not a race, so take

the time to enjoy the planning and the construction of each page and spread.

① ORGANIZE PHOTOS

Your photos have already been sorted by either date or theme and stored in photo-safe containers. Now it's time to pull them out and re-sort them into smaller categories or groupings, as shown. Decide which photos you wish to feature on the pages of your current album project—in this case, a college theme album. Set them aside and put away the others.

② LAY OUT PAGES

Determine what photos will appear on which pages using the worksheet on page 96. (If necessary refer to your sketches on the page design worksheet on page 63.) These rough sketches represent the pages of your scrapbook and act as a preliminary blueprint for the placement of your photos. When using the sketches to plan your layout, make sure to leave room for journaling. Build in extra room for the display of photos you wish to have enlarged. The number and sizes of photos you are going to use will determine the size of the album you need to purchase and the number of pages you will create.

③ PURCHASE AN ALBUM

Take your photos and sketched layouts with you to the store to purchase an album, refill pages and page protectors. When selecting the album, consider the size and shape of the items you will be displaying. Consider purchasing extra pages so that you can spread your layouts if you find your photos look too crowded. You can always return unopened packages of pages and page protectors if you find you do not need them. Put photos inside page protectors to "hold" space on those spreads as shown.

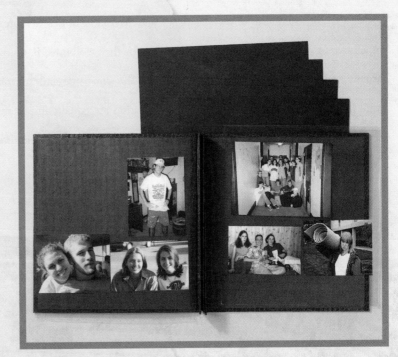

④ PURCHASE PAPER AND ACCESSORIES

With your new album and photos in hand, you will find it much easier to select paper colors and page accessories—stickers, die cuts, stamps, pen colors and more. Select papers and a few simple design elements based on your primary color scheme and carry the theme, color and style throughout your book to help tie your pages together and create a feeling of unity.

Creating album continuity

Just as the consistent use of colored paper and page accessories tie spreads together, they are imperative for creating a cohesive look and feel for theme albums. Borders can act as bookends, visually embracing sections of your scrapbook. The same title and cropping treatments further unite pages. The journaling "voice" and presentation are equally important in creating a tightly woven scrapbook. On the following pages you'll find examples of scrapbooks that have it all— cohesion, clarity, continuity and creativity.

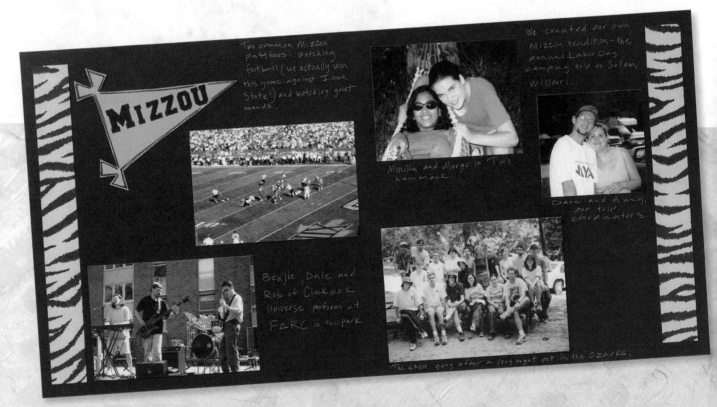

The selection of black pages for this leather album is a good choice, as black is one of the University's official colors.

COLLEGE ALBUM While the University of Missouri alum that created this album had no control over the colors appearing in the photos, she could control other colors within the scrapbook. Her paper choice reflects the University's official colors: black and gold. The patterned border recalls the college mascot—a tiger. Through consistent use of these colors and embellishments, she created a cohesive look.

Repetitive use of one simple design element—a free-hand-cut paper pennant bearing the college moniker—helps carry this album's theme throughout its pages.

Journaling in the same gold pen on every page ties the pages together and creates a feeling of consistency.

Photos Kimberly Ball, Denver, Colorado

SPORTS ALBUM It is hard to strike out when you tie your album pages together with style. These baseball pages hit a design home run. Consistent paper colors unite each spread. If you plan to create a sports album that encompasses different sports and different sport seasons, consider using a new paper choice for each to help differentiate them.

BASEBALL BUILDS CHARACTER

2001

11 and 12 year old
Fayetteville
All Star
Team

Coaches: Todd Gaskill, Monty Hall, Scotty St...
Players: Clay Gill, Tyler Shelton, Blake Dorris, Cody Gask...
Brandon Netherland, Chris Mitchell, Rob Gray, Matthe...
Barnes, Chris Shelton, Antwon Brown, Freddie...

Handmade especially for you by C. Gray — Character Quality Clu...

We're a Team!

FAITH VS PRESUMPTION
Confidence that actions rooted in good character will yield the best outcome, even when I cannot see how.

HUMILITY VS PRIDE
ACKNOWLEDGING THAT ACHIEVEMENT RESULTS FROM THE INVESTMENT OF God and others in my life.

Honor   Humility   Initiative

Repetitive use of matted page titles, computer fonts and pen stroke stitching on the journaling blocks further support this album's continuation of theme and design.

Cathy Gray, Fayetteville, Tennessee

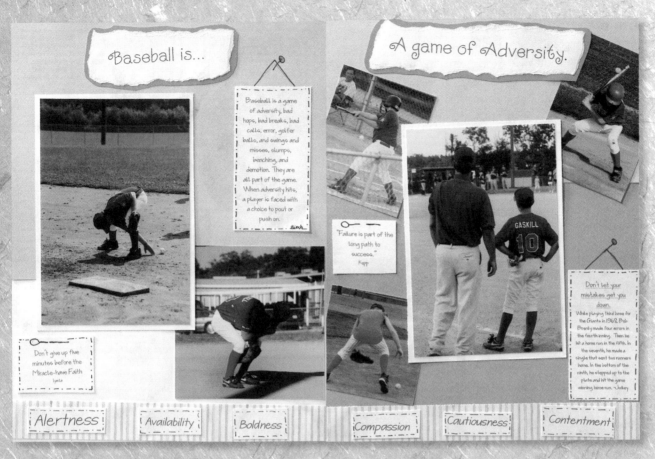

Baseball is...

A game of Adversity.

Baseball is a game of adversity, bad hops, bad breaks, bad calls, error, golfer balls, and swings and misses, slumps, benching, and demotion. They are all part of the game. When adversity hits, a player is faced with a choice to pout or push on. —Dierk

"Failure is part of the long path to success." Kipp

GASKILL 10

Don't give up five minutes before the Miracle–have Faith Lynda

Don't let your mistakes get you down.
While playing third base for the Giants in 1962, Bob Brenly made four errors in the fourth inning. Then he hit a home run in the fifth. In the seventh, he made a single that sent two runners home. In the bottom of the ninth, he stepped up to the plate and hit the game winning home run. —Jubley

| Alertness | Availability | Boldness | Compassion | Cautiousness | Contentment |

Consistent photo treatments and patterned paper border along the pages' lower edges give this album its crisp, clean, "pulled together" look.

The Importance of Saying Thank you...

Wisdom vs. Foolishness
Making practical applications of truth in daily decisions

"It breaks your heart. It is designed to break your heart. The game begins in the spring, when everything else begins again, and it blossoms in the summer, filling the afternoons and evenings, and then as soon as the chill rains come, it stops and leaves you to face the fall alone. You count on it, rely on it to buffer the passage of time, to keep the memory of sunshine and high skies alive, and then just when the days are all twilight, when you need it most, it stops." Giamatti

GENEROSITY vs. STINGINESS
CAREFULLY MANAGING MY RESOURCES SO I CAN FREELY GIVE TO THOSE IN NEED.

| Determination | Diligence | Discernment | Creativity | Decisiveness | Enthusiasm |

HERITAGE ALBUM These heritage photos are united on pages that share unique design elements. While the market offers an amazing array of gorgeous heritage-themed papers and accessories, beautiful pages can also be created with the paper you may already own and a few simple accessories.

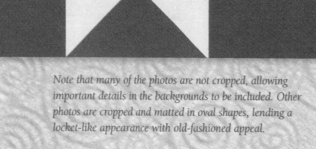

Note that many of the photos are not cropped, allowing important details in the backgrounds to be included. Other photos are cropped and matted in oval shapes, lending a locket-like appearance with old-fashioned appeal.

These pages successfully carry the theme and look of antique quilts. Pen stroke stitching, done in black ink, details and supports the quilted backdrops on which the photos are displayed.

Debra Fee, Broomfield, Colorado

Hatch

Etta

Ina

Maud

Edna

daughters of
Nora Ella
and
David

Friends

The following pages contain a sampling of the many photographs my grandmother treasured over the years. They were never labeled, because the names that went with these faces were etched in her heart. I have included them here because they reflect a time and culture that should never be forgotten.

Charlie Rogers   Elmer Hatch

Thumbnail sketches work sheet

Thumbnail sketches, which are nothing more than mini versions of pages in the album, can help you visualize the number of album pages you have to fill. Use this work sheet to help plan the order of your scrapbook. Begin by photocopying this page. Then group the photos and memorabilia you plan to place on each page. Order the groupings as you would have them appear in the album, beginning with the first page or spread and moving toward the back of the book. Once you're satisfied with the album's layout, write or draw in the page progression on the work sheet below.

TITLE PAGE

ENDING PAGE

Including memorabilia in your album

Memorabilia is often as important to scrapbookers as their photos. However, including those

newspaper clippings, old documents and certificates, maps, postcards, letters, invitations, coins,

pressed flowers, locks of hair and other keepsakes in albums poses some challenges. A lot of

memorabilia is acidic and, as such, is not photo-safe. But with a little ingenuity, planning and the

right supplies, photos and memorabilia can live happily side by side within your album.

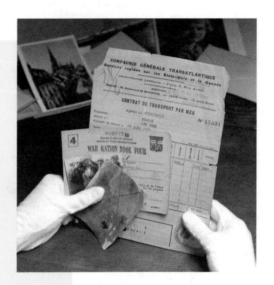

MEMORABILIA PRESERVATION TIPS

- Photocopy old documents, certificates, and newspaper clippings onto acid- and lignin-free paper. Use the copies in your album. Store additional memorabilia in an archival-quality memorabilia box.

- Encapsulate deacidified or fragile memorabilia items.

- Never allow memorabilia and photos to touch.

- When placing photos and memorabilia in close proximity, create barriers between the two. Mats help keep acids in memorabilia from migrating to photos.

- Photograph bulky memorabilia such as trophies or corsages and include the pictures in your album.

- Place memorabilia in archival-quality envelopes and attach the envelopes directly to your page.

- Mount memorabilia with nonpermanent techniques such as self-adhesive photo corners so that you can easily remove the pieces to view or copy later.

- When handling old documents, wear cotton gloves to prevent damage from skin oils and dirt.

To neutralize (de-acidify) the acids in paper such as newspaper, certificates or cards, spray with a buffering spritz. To treat paper with Archival Mist™, shake the bottle vigorously and follow the pumping directions on the container. Apply spray lightly and evenly 6" from the paper's surface on both sides of the paper and allow to dry before adhering. When treating papers containing chalk or pastels, spray the reverse side only.

Memorabilia encapsulation methods

There are a number of convenient ways to encapsulate memorabilia so it can be safely displayed in your scrapbook. Encapsulation makes it possible to include photos and memorabilia on the same pages without damaging the photos. Encapsulation systems come in a variety of sizes and include transparent plastic sleeves, keepers and pockets. Make sure the product you choose is PVC-free and made from polyethylene, polypropylene or polyester.

Plastic keepers, available in different shapes, are good for storing 3-D memorabilia, such as coins and lockets of hair.

Pam Klassen, Denver Colorado

ENCAPSULATION TIPS

- Use memorabilia keepers, sleeves or envelopes to encapsulate organic items such as pressed flowers, leaves, sand and tiny shells.

- Use encapsulation systems to display metallic items such as coins and keys. Metallic items generally do not pose a chemical risk to scrapbooks unless they contain iron. Copper also has a tendency to corrode.

- Use pockets or envelopes to encapsulate hair, fur, feathers or other similar items.

- Use sleeves to display and protect paper memorabilia such as de-acidified birth certificates, postcards or recipe cards.

- Use sleeves and pockets to encapsulate maps, playbills and other bulky pieces of paper memorabilia.

HOW TO MAKE A POCKET PAGE

Pocket pages are easy to make and provide a safe environment for flat memorabilia such as certificates, cards, schedules and other documents. You can use decorative rulers or scissors to make different cuts along the top of the pocket. Decorate with stickers, die cuts, stamps or punch art that relate to the theme of the pocket's contents.

1 *Use a decorative ruler and a pencil to draw a line across the center of a sheet of card-stock. The cardstock should be the same size as the paper used for the page background. Cut along line with scissors to create piece for "pocket."*

2 *Attach double-sided tape adhesive to the back of the "pocket" along the two sides and the lower edge, keeping the upper edge of the pocket adhesive-free.*

3 *Mount pocket onto scrapbook page along lower edge and sides. Accent as desired and fill with memorabilia.*

Special Christmas

Memories

2001

Each year before we open gifts at Grandma and Grandpa Gerbrandt's we read the Christmas story from the Bible (Luke). Now that all three kids are old enough they all want to get a piece of the action. This was Daniel's first year to read. He is doing so amazing with his reading.

Grandpa Gordon   Anna   Sasha   Daniel
      67   11   9   6

Journaling

It is the combination of words and pictures that give scrapbooks long-lasting value. I learned the importance of journaling the hard way...by looking back at my early books and realizing I simply had not included enough information. I found myself wondering who the people in the pictures were and where the photos had been taken.

While some scrapbookers are as comfortable putting words on paper as they are pictures and embellishments, others have to learn the art of journaling. Often, that means ridding themselves of preconceptions about what constitutes good writing. Scrapbook journaling isn't about dotting your "I's" and crossing your "T's." Nor is it about sentence structure or perfect paragraphs. It is about sharing important information and special stories.

I've heard every excuse in the book from those who do not journal. This chapter will address them and offer ways to work through your concerns. So pick up your pen and get ready to learn to write right!

LIKE MANY SCRAPBOOKERS, I FIRST FELL IN LOVE WITH THE ART OF PAGE DESIGN. IT HAS TAKEN SOME TIME, BUT THROUGH THE YEARS I'VE TRAINED MYSELF TO BECOME A COMPETENT JOURNALER.

–Michele

What to say

Scrapbook journaling isn't about how much you write. It is about the quality of information you share. Well-journaled scrapbook pages include information that reinforces the visuals by "telling" rather than "showing" what is displayed on the page.

While you may wish to include journaled jokes, stories and insights, you must also include some basic information such as what is happening in the pictures, who appears, and where, and when the event unfolded. How extensively you address these questions is up to you, but the bare facts are imperative. Well-journaled pages are like well-written storybooks. They leave the reader feeling content, as though all the pieces fell into place and the package was tied up with a tidy bow.

MAKE IT YOUR OWN

- Include the basic facts: what, when, who and where.

- Use your journaling to tell "the rest of the story."

- Describe how you felt and the mood of the occasion.

- Add a poem, quote or saying that illustrates the page's theme.

- Include the thoughts, feelings and words of those who shared the event.

- Share snippets of conversation or jokes.

INSUFFICIENT JOURNALING

WHAT?
What is going on in the pictures? What event is taking place? What was being said? What happened before and after the shot was taken? What inspired the expressions?

WHEN?
What day, month and year were these photos taken? Was this a special holiday or celebration?

WHO?
Who are the people in the photos? What are their names? Are they friends or relatives? Who was at the event who didn't get included in the photos?

WHERE?
Where did the event take place? Why was this location important? How was it chosen?

EFFECTIVE JOURNALING

A well-journaled page will be as pertinent to readers decades from now as it is in the present. They will be able to enjoy the pages more because the questions they might raise have been answered. They are able to see the scrapbooked events in a context that makes the page more compelling.

Sasha's 8th Birthday

June 16, 2000
We celebrated Sasha's birthday at Bana and Pop-Pop's new home.
Bana, Sasha, Anna, Daniel, Katie & Pop Pop.

We had fun playing games, then opened many wonderful presents and had cake and ice cream. One of her favorite cousins, Katie Blessing was able to stay with us the whole weekend to help us celebrate.

Getting the facts

Before you begin to write, you need to know what to write. Sometimes the information is readily available. Other times you may feel as though you're trying to spin words from air because the facts have blurred in your memory. Or, perhaps you simply never knew the facts. This is especially true when working on projects such as a heritage album. There are many ways to claim the information you need. The Internet is a terrific resource and there are dozens of books that can guide you through the process of uncovering family history. Through the creation of your scrapbooks you are answering the questions that may be so important to future generations.

KEEP A JOURNAL

The human mind too often resembles a sieve. Names, dates, jokes, quotes, facts and figures run out and away almost as quickly as they are inputted. And no matter how often you tell yourself, "Oh, I'll certainly remember THAT," you just don't. Which is why it's a good idea to keep a small journal and pencil in your purse or car whenever you step out. Start making a point to jot down notes each time you pull out your camera. Include adjectives that will help you remember sights, sounds, smells and tastes. Include the date so you can later match journaled information to your pictures. If you don't keep a daily journal, holding on to your kitchen calendars can also help you "fill in the blanks" where photo information is concerned.

WHERE TO TURN FOR HISTORICAL INFORMATION

- Ask family members and friends about their memories.

- Look in family Bibles in which dates of weddings, births and deaths may be noted.

- Read old family letters and diaries.

- Visit cemeteries in which family members were buried.

- Search newspapers for references to family members.

- Find school yearbooks. If you don't have a copy, contact the school.

- Ferret out family papers such as wedding and death certificates, mortgage papers, portfolios, military commendations, household accounts, receipts, income tax statements and driver's licenses.

- Talk to religious leaders in communities in which family members lived.

- Contact and join a genealogical or historical society in the area in which you are interested.

- Use U.S. census information. Pick up a genealogy book in order to find out how to access it.

- Search county courthouse records for information about weddings, divorces, property records, wills and deeds.

INTERVIEWING

Helping others open the doors to their memories can be a challenge, but once you've mastered the technique you'll have friends and relatives sharing their most cherished stories. Brainstorm a list of questions before the interview. Include more than you may need so you can skip those that seem less pertinent while conducting the interview. Good interviewers never ask questions that can be answered with a simple "yes" or "no." Instead, they ask leading questions that begin with words such as, "why" and "how" (example: Why did you decide to move to Texas? How did you feel about the move?). While conducting the interview, focus your attention on your subject. Respond to answers by nodding, adding verbal affirmations, and laughing if something is funny. Be sure to give your subject adequate time to reply. Keep note taking to a minimum, writing down "memory joggers" and facts such as dates and names. You may wish to use a tape recorder. End the session when your subject tires.

QUESTIONS TO GET THEM TALKING

- What is your favorite song or poem and why?

- How did you feel when you found out you were going to be a parent?

- How did your family celebrate holidays?

- How do you want to be remembered?

- How would you describe yourself?

- How would you like others to describe you?

- If you could talk to your descendants 100 years from now, what would you tell them?

- Of what are you most proud and why?

- What was your childhood like?

- What world event stands out most strongly in your memory?

- What life choice would you change if you knew then what you know now?

- What have been the happiest and saddest events in your life?

- If you could spend the evening with one famous person—past or present—who would it be and why would you choose him?

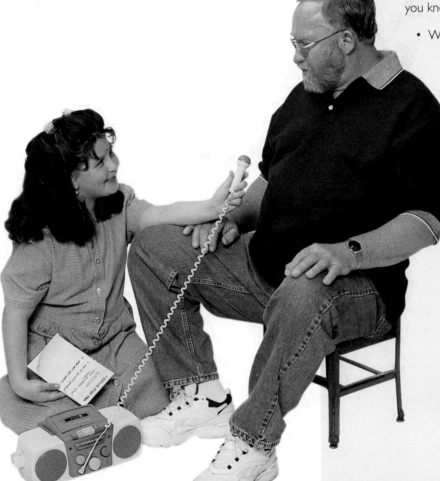

Overcoming journaling fears

Many people suffer from journaling jitters. Some find themselves pulling a complete blank when they look at an empty page. Others develop sweaty palms and shaking hands the minute they pick up a pen. Many jittery writers have been sent, at some time in their lives, the message that their writing isn't up to par. Years later, they are still afraid to put words on paper for fear they won't say the right thing or won't say it the right way. If this describes you, it is time to put aside your concerns and move forward. Here are some tips and tricks to turn timid journalers into pros.

I HATE MY HANDWRITING

Handwriting is as individual as the person writing the words. It says a lot about the times in which we live. Different periods throughout history have placed more importance on penmanship than others, and popular styles of penmanship have been embraced over the years.

There is something compelling about old letters handwritten by long-gone family members. The rigid formality of some, the uneven swoops and swirls of others, and the ink splotches and doodles say as much about the writer as the letter's content.

For these reasons, many scrapbooking experts advocate journaling with a pen, rather than a computer. But if you simply can't live comfortably with your handwriting, invest in one of the many font CDs on the market. They allow you to select from a library of fonts, change their colors, sizes and even fill pattern. Print your message on photo-safe paper and apply to your page.

MISTAKE FIXERS

- Wite Out® over the mistake. Rewrite directly on top of the Wite Out.

- Cover the mistake with another piece of paper cut or punched into a decorative shape.

- Cut or tear paper into shapes. Layer the pieces to create design elements that can cover mistakes.

- Save scraps from cropped pictures. Use the pieces to patch problem areas.

- Use stickers, die cuts and shapes punched from photo scraps to cover mistakes.

HELP FOR MESSY JOURNALING

Clean and pleasant-looking journaling is often the result of planning. It is best to place your photos and decorative elements on your scrapbook page before you begin to write. Then, using a ruler, draw straight guidelines along which you can journal. Journaling templates are also wonderful tools that help prevent words from weaving and wandering arbitrarily across a page. Try templates with waves, spirals and zigzag lines to break up linear text. Simply align the template on your page or paper and trace the lines in ink or vanishing ink. Add your journaling along the lines.

Journaling templates are a dream come true for scrapbookers. They provide guidelines which the writer can follow to ensure tidy journaling.

ADD ZING TO YOUR WORDS

- Turn certain letters into tiny illustrations. If you are writing about pizza, for example, turn the letter "A" into a mini slice. Or turn the "O" in the word "balloon" into a balloon.

- Write text and then embellish the dots above the letter "i" with stickers. Add stickers to the ends of sentences instead of periods.

- Write the first letter in a block of text larger than the rest of the text.

- Emphasize key words in sentences by making them bigger, bolder, or by changing their color.

- Write your messages on pretty journaling stickers, or use journaling stickers with pre-printed messages.

Journaling stickers and cutouts are printed with or without lines upon which you can journal. These are available in a variety of styles, sizes and themes. Some stickers are pre-printed with messages.

Types of journaling

There are many different ways to present journaling on your scrapbook pages. Some methods are direct and to the point. Others are more free flowing and creative. The type of journaling you select will be determined by a number of factors including your level of comfort with the written word and the theme and mood of your page. It will also be impacted by the amount you want to say, and the amount of room you have to say it in. On the following pages you'll find ideas for ways to include journaling in your album. Remember that journaling is a part of your page design and how you present it can be as important as what you say.

BULLET JOURNALING

Bullet journaling is a quick-and-easy way to address the facts without having to wrap text in sentences and paragraphs. Bullets supply basic information such as who, what, when and where the photos were taken.

KID CONVERSATION STARTERS

Bullet-style journaling is the perfect way to add charm to a Father's Day (or Mother's Day) gift album. The album can be illustrated with casual photos, formal portraits, children's artwork, stickers and more. Some of the conversation starters used to inspire the children's comments in the journaled page below include:

- Daddy and I are different because...
- Daddy and I are the same because...
- Daddy and I like to sing and our favorite song is...
- Daddy is like [name an animal] because...
- Daddy is silly when he...
- Daddy likes it when...
- I love Daddy as much as...
- I wish Daddy would...
- My favorite time with Daddy was...
- Our favorite thing Daddy does with us is...
- We have most fun as a family when...
- We like it when...
- What Daddy does at work is...
- What I do when Daddy is at work is...

Laurie Connolly, Mukilteo, Washington

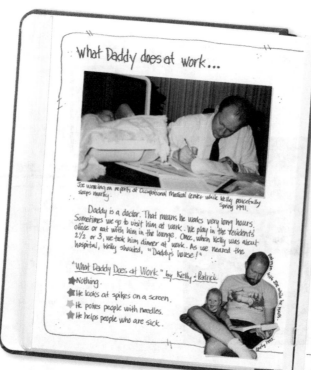

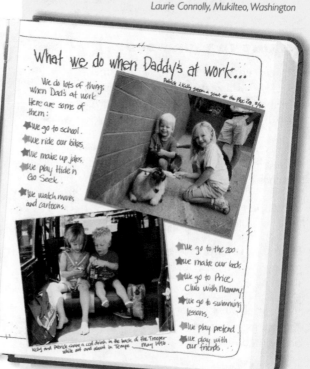

SHORT CAPTION JOURNALING

So much can be conveyed in so few words! Short caption journaling is a way of telling the story briefly and concisely. Include in the captions those basic facts about who, where, what and when and then add a few interesting details. Don't feel like you need to go to town constructing elaborate tomes. Just say what you need to say and move on.

Lifelong friendships and the shared experience of braces prompted this snapshot. Its short caption quickly hits upon what's going on in the photos without sacrificing too much detail.

Karen Regep Glover
Grosse Pointe Woods, Michigan

PERSPECTIVE JOURNALING

Perspective journaling reflects not just the memories, thoughts and feelings of the scrapbooker, but also the impressions of others. Begin adding perspective journaling to your albums by asking family members and friends to write about their thoughts on momentous occasions. If they prefer, they may wish to dictate to you. Do not feel as though you need pages of reflections from each person; a few sentences will do just fine. The more perspectives you include, the more "voices" you add to your album.

Siblings are famous for having very different memories of certain events as documented by this page featuring three sisters who clearly remember different things about Christmases past.

Photos Deborah Mock, Denver, Colorado

POETIC JOURNALING

Poetic journaling utilizes published songs, book titles, poems, stories, quotes, sayings and Bible verses. Or you can write your own poems that reflect the sentiment depicted on a scrapbook page. It can rhyme or be free verse. Poetic journaling is a natural choice for historical, holiday, wedding, anniversary, travel and children's theme albums.

Poetic journaling can be as simple as a sentimental saying.

Photos Ken Trujillo

BRING YOUR JOURNALING ALIVE

Use descriptive words that help capture the mood. A dictionary or thesaurus will offer even more great adjectives.

Adventuresome	Fragrant	Keen	Parched	Unassuming
Artistic	Frosty	Knobby	Pungent	Uncanny
Beautiful	Gooey	Legendary	Quick	Valorous
Bitter	Graceful	Loving	Quiet	Velvety
Creative	Happy-go-lucky	Magical	Restless	Waterlogged
Crisp	Homespun	Musty	Rousing	Wayward
Delectable	Icy	Naughty	Scraggly	Yippy
Downy	Irresistible	Nimble	Smooth	Yummy
Edgy	Jaunty	Original	Testy	Zingy
Elegant	Jolly	Outgoing	Trendy	Zippy

Poetry made simple work sheet

If you can't find a poem that says it all, write one yourself. These simple, fill-in-the-blank formulas—one a sentimental poem, the other, a lighter limerick—will give your pages poetic justice in no time!

SENTIMENTAL POEM EXAMPLE

My Beautiful One
By Susan Smith

Rose
Giggly, curious, dreamy, musical
Loves dancing, spinning and whirling
Hates math, cruelty, repetition
Yearns for adventure, love and fame
Shares with the world laughter and hope
Will certainly follow her heart
Without whom I would fade away
Rose
My lovely daughter.

Title of Poem _____

Author's Name _____

_____ (a person's name)

_____ , _____ , _____ , _____

(four words that describe the person's character)

Loves _____ , _____ and _____

Hates _____ , _____ , _____

Yearns for _____ , _____ and _____

Shares with the world _____ and _____

Will certainly_____

Without whom I _____

_____ (the person's name again)

My _____

LIGHTER LIMERICK POEM EXAMPLE

A limerick is a five-lined verse. The limerick is structured so that lines one, two and five all rhyme. Lines three and four rhyme. A limerick rocks along like a cantering horse with a da-da-DUM rhythm. Each of these da-da-DUM patterns is called a metric foot. Lines one, two and five of the limerick must have exactly three metric feet. Lines three and four must have exactly two metric feet. The first foot of each line may just start out with a da-DUM rather than a da-da-DUM. Good limericks have a final line that is especially clever.

There ONCE was a DOG known as RO-ver
Who RAN out to PLAY in the CLO-ver
Though once COV-ered with SPOTS—
He got BURNED 'tween the DOTS—
And NOW he looks SUN-tanned all OVER.

_____

_____

_____

_____

_____

_____

_____

_____

_____

_____

STORYTELLING JOURNALING

Storytelling journaling steps beyond the basic information and delves into the history behind pictures and memorabilia. It tends to take on a narrative voice that involves the reader, much like a novel. Similar to a novel, storytelling journaling often calls on the senses of sight, smell, sound and touch to establish and carry a mood. Text from storytelling tends to be a bit longer and descriptions are more intricate.

Accented with just a silhouette-cropped and matted photo and a simple stamped border, the story of a giving soul is captured.

Michele Rank
Cerritos, California

GOOD STORYTELLING TIPS

- Write like you speak.

- Tape record the story as you tell it to a friend or family member. Transcribe it later.

- Remember that all good stories have a beginning, middle and end.

- Choose a story beginning that sets the mood and captures the reader's attention.

- Allow the story's middle to move the plot forward logically.

- Make sure the end of the story wraps up the tale and leaves the reader feeling content.

- Use powerful adjectives and strong verbs and adverbs.

- Most good stories (like the *Wizard of Oz*) have a heroine/hero who wants or needs something. On her way to achieving it she runs into obstacles. Through wit and bravery she overcomes them and gets her reward. Consider building your journaled story using the same format.

- Don't be afraid to include the good, the bad and the ugly in your story.

REBUS JOURNALING

Rebus journaling involves using both words and tiny pictures in a sentence. The pictures can either replace a word or reinforce it. For example, the letter "I" at the beginning of a phrase may be replaced with a picture of a human eye. The word "love" may be replaced with a heart. Or, you may wish to write the word "love" and place a tiny heart just after it, as an illustration. Rebus journaling takes some time and thought, but pays off in truly unique pages.

A form of rebus storytelling (pictures within journaling) helps to preserve this birthday story.

Julie Labuszewski, Littleton, Colorado

Making room for journaling

Journaling is as important to a successful scrapbook page as photos and memorabilia, but too many scrapbookers fail to consider journaling space when designing their spreads. Only after their photos and decorative items have been adhered do they realize that there is simply no room left on the page for writing. Do not get caught in this bind. Plan ahead and remember that journaling can run across the top or bottom of the page, down the sides in columns, or flow around photos. It may sit atop die cuts or be written on a separate sheet of paper and tucked behind photo mats. With a little ingenuity you can find the means and the space to add a few well-chosen words to even crowded pages.

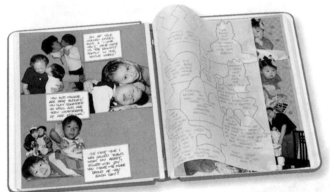

Stacey Shigaya, Denver, Colorado

Vellum is an ideal material for creating overlays for journaling. The translucent quality of vellum allows you to place your journaling directly over a photo. Sketch the basic layout of your page on a sheet of vellum. Add journaling and then slip the overlay into an empty page protector and insert it in front of the corresponding page.

GO AROUND IT

Journal around photos, directly on the scrapbook page or on the photo mats. Journaling around photo mats is a simple solution for adding words when it seems like there is really no room for them.

Photos Sally Scamfer, Bellvue, Nebraska

EXTEND IT

Page extenders, sold in a number of different styles by different manufacturers, supply additional room on which to journal. Some extenders
are conjoined page protectors. When closing your album you simply
fold the extended page or pages back into the book.

Creative titles and lettering

Every successful scrapbook page must have a title. Like the headline on the front page of a newspaper, the title loudly declares what has taken place and prepares the reader for the material that will follow. Subsequent titles help steer the reader from one topic to another. The title is often placed on the top of a page like a banner, but may also run down the side or sit in the middle of a page. The title can be straight forward or catchy. From a design perspective, the title should coordinate with the other visual elements on the page. Titles can be created with computer fonts or drawn freehand. They can also be made with stickers, punches or stamps.

CREATIVE LETTERING IDEAS

When the urge hits and the page calls for it, put down the pen and pick up these tools and supplies in order to create dynamic titles.

PUNCHES & SMALL DIE CUTS Lettering punches and small die cuts are available in upper- and lowercase and various styles.

STICKERS Stickers come in a plethora of shapes and colors and are available in multiple fonts and themes.

STAMPS Letter stamps are available in upper- and lowercase and in a multitude of fonts. Personalize stamped letters by filling them in with different colors or embossing over them.

TEMPLATES Lettering templates help you create jumbo or mini letters in styles that run from whimsical to elegant.

COMPUTER FONTS Today's computer-savvy scrapbooker can choose from a number of commercial software programs that offer designer fonts with varying degrees of manipulation.

MIX AND MATCH FOR A ONE-OF-A-KIND TITLE LOOK

Let these titles jump-start your imagination. Make them your own by creatively combining different tools, papers and colors in one page title.

BEST FRIENDS *combines letter stickers and letters traced with a template.*

SUMMER DAYS *is made up of photo die cuts and stamped letters.*

HAPPY BIRTHDAY *is layered with tiny punched letters atop letter stickers.*

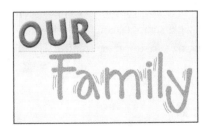

OUR LOVE UNITES US *mixes stamped letters with letter fonts.*

OUR FAMILY *was made with letter stickers and a journaling font.*

TERRIFIC TITLE IDEAS

BABY
Born to Be Wild
Cute as a Button
Diaper Daze
Special Delivery
Sugar and Spice and
  Everything Nice

CAREER
For It's Work All Day
  For the Sugar in Your Tea
Happiness Comes From a Job
  Well Done
Takin' Care of Business
Whistle While You Work
Workin' For a Living

CELEBRATIONS
Celebrate Good Times,
  Come On, Celebrate!
Happy Birthday
Party Down
The More the Merrier
We're All Together Again

COLLEGE
Goin' Places
Got Computer, Will Travel
I've Got Class
Party Animal
Student on Bored

FRIENDS
Family and Friends Are
  Life's Gifts
Friends Forever
Kindred Spirits
When Friends Meet,
  Hearts Warm
You Make My Heart Smile

HERITAGE
From Strong Roots Grow
  Lovely Branches
It's All Relative
Our Family Tree is Full of Nuts
Through the Ages
We Honor the Past

HOBBY
An Artist is Born
Better Sorry Than Safe
Craftaholic in Residence
I Am Creative, Not Tidy!
If It Does Not Move, Paint It

HOLIDAY
A Cause for Celebration
Kick Up Your Heels
Merry Christmas
Rejoice
Santa's Little Helpers

PETS
A Real Stable Pony
Fish Tales
For the Birds
It is the Cats Meow
Love Some Bunny
There is a Mouse in the House
To Err is Human,
  To Forgive, Canine

SCHOOL DAYS
Best Buddies 4 Ever
Hard at Work
Mad Science
Just a Swingin'
Kids Do the Darndest Things

SEASONS
April Showers Bring
  May Flowers
Fall Forward
Leaf the Raking to Dad
Let It Snow!
Sizzlin' Summertime Fun
Welcome Winter
You Are My Sunshine

SPORTS
Bad Losers Good Winners
Have a Ball
If First You Don't Succeed
  Try, Try Again
Kickin'
My Special Hotshot

TODDLER
Here Comes Trouble
I Spy
Make A Wish
No! No! No!
Preschool Daze
Warning, Kids At Play

TRAVEL
Destination Relaxation
Get Out the Map
If You Come to a Fork
  in the Road, Take It
The Journey Not the
  Destination, Matters
What a Wonderful World
Wish You Were Here

WEDDING
Fairy Tale Romance
Happily Ever After
I Do
On the Wings of Love
We Unite With Joyful Hearts

Where to go from here

You have come to the end of a new adventure—the creation of your first precious album and the conclusion of this book. But you are just beginning your journey as a lifelong scrapbooker. Along the way you'll meet many people who share your hobby. They will also share ideas and information that will help you grow as a preserver of memories. Enjoy making new friends as you join the worldwide community of scrapbookers.

CLASSES

Find out about scrapbooking classes by visiting your local craft or scrapbook store. Additional information can be found on numerous scrapbooking Web sites. Most stores hosting classes charge a nominal fee. Call or stop by to find out what scrapbooking topic they have planned. Classes fill up quickly; be sure to preregister.

COMPUTER

Your computer is one of your most valuable assets. Use it for genealogy research; visit the countless scrapbook product Web sites to comparison shop or locate hard-to-find items, scan, manipulate and print images; download free fonts and clip art for pages. Chat online with other scrapbookers willing to share similar concerns and to exchange ideas and tips. Use these keywords for successful searching: scrapbook, scrapbooking, scrapbook consultants, genealogy and free downloads.

CONVENTIONS

Scrapbook conventions are a great place to learn new techniques from scrapbook professionals and to pick up tips from fellow classmates. Most fill quickly, though, so be sure to preregister. Many activities are listed in scrapbooking magazines, including *Memory Makers*.

CRAFT AND SCRAPBOOK STORES

Besides attending classes and crops, you will want to visit these to stay stocked up for scrapbooking and to keep posted on the latest and greatest products, tools, tips and techniques. Sometimes there is no better motivator to get scrapbooking than visiting a scrapbook store!

All My Memories, Llittleton, Colorado

CROPS

Many craft and scrapbook stores host crops. Or form your own crop club to make new scrapping friends by running an ad in your local or school paper. You can also post a "Scrappers Wanted" notice on the bulletin board of your local scrapbooking store letting others know that you are looking to meet fellow scrapbookers to share ideas and swap tools and supplies.

LIBRARY OR BOOKSTORE

If you like to browse before you buy, visit your local public library or bookstore to check out the many inspiring scrapbook-related magazines and books on the market. If your library does not carry such publications, a few customer requests for them may prompt the library to obtain them.

Illustrated glossary of scrapbook terms and techniques

ACCESSORIES

Page accents that you can make or buy. Can include stickers, die cuts, stamped images and punch art. May also include baubles (beads, buttons, rhinestones, sequins), colorants (pens, chalk, inkpads), metallics (charms, wire, jewelry-making components, eyelets, fasteners), textiles (ribbon, embroidery floss, thread), or organics (raffia, pressed flowers and leaves, tiny shells, sand). With all of the latter, small and flat are best. See pages 55 and 71.

ACID-FREE

Look for scrapbook products—particularly pages, paper, adhesives and inks—that are free from harmful acids that can eat away at the emulsion on your photos. Harmful acids can occur in the manufacturing process. Check labels for "acid-free" and "photo-safe." See pages 10 and 24.

ADHESIVES

Products used to adhere or attach photos, accessories and memorabilia to scrapbook pages. Buy and use only acid-free and photo-safe adhesives in a scrapbook. See pages 28-29.

ALBUM

The archival-quality book in which you place your finished scrapbook pages for posterity and for safekeeping. Magnetic albums can destroy photos and memorabilia; remove items and place in safer albums. See pages 10 and 22-23.

ARCHIVAL QUALITY

A nontechnical term suggesting that a substance is chemically stable, durable and permanent. For archival qualities related to specific materials see page 10.

BALANCE

A harmonious or satisfying arrangement or proportion of photos and elements on a scrapbook page. See pages 54 and 60-63.

BORDER

The upper, lower and side edges or margins of a scrapbook page. Sometimes refers to a border design that is handmade or manufactured and attached to a page. See page 74.

BUFFERED PAPER

Paper in which certain alkaline substances have been added during the manufacturing process to prevent acids from forming in the future due to chemical reactions. See pages 10 and 24.

CARDSTOCK

The heaviest of scrapbook papers; can be solid-colored or patterned. Best for page backgrounds and pocket pages. See pages 24 and 99.

CD-ROM

A compact disc that can store large amounts of digitized photos and data files. In scrapbooking, font and lettering CDs as well as scrapbook software CDs can be helpful in the page-making process. See pages 51 and 106.

CHRONOLOGICAL

Arranged in order of time of occurrence as it pertains to the sorting and organizing of photos and memorabilia or the order in which photos and memorabilia appear in an album. See pages 78-81.

CONTINUITY

The state or quality of being continuous or a sense of that which is uninterrupted as in continuous or uninterrupted flow of pages in an album. See pages 74-75 and 90-95.

CROP

An event attended by scrapbookers for the purpose of scrapbooking, sharing ideas and tools and swapping products; held at conventions, craft and scrapbook stores and in private homes. See page 119.

CROPPING

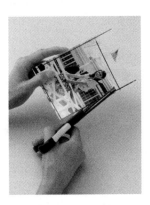

The act of cutting or trimming photos to enhance the image, eliminate unnecessary backgrounds or turn the photos into unique works of art. See pages 55 and 64-68.

DE-ACIDIFY

To chemically treat paper memorabilia to neutralize acids while applying an alkaline buffer to discourage further acid migration from damaging photos. See page 97.

DECORATIVE SCISSORS

Scissors with special-cut blades or teeth that provide a wide array of cut patterns and designs, available in various cutting depths. Flipping decorative scissors over will result in a varied cutting pattern. See page 30.

DESIGN

A visual composition or pattern of photos, journaling and accessories that ultimately become a finished scrapbook page. See pages 54 and 60-63.

DIE CUTS

The resulting paper or photograph letter or shape cut with a die that is rolled through a die-cut machine; a page accessory. See page 36.

DIGITAL

A computer-related term for the process of using numerical digits to create uniform photographic images as shot with a digital camera or scanned into a computer with a scanner and saved on and retrieved from a CD-ROM. See page 51.

ENCAPSULATE

To encase paper or three-dimensional memorabilia in PVC-free plastic sleeves, envelopes and keepers for its own preservation and the protection of your photos. See page 98.

JOURNALING

Refers to handwritten, handmade or computer-generated text that provides pertinent details about what is taking place in photographs. See pages 101-117.

LAYOUT

To put or spread out photos and memorabilia in readiness for scrapbooking or a sketch of a scrapbook page design. See pages 54 and 60-63.

LETTERING

The act of forming or creating letters to use in scrapbook page titles and journaling. Lettering can include freehand cut or drawn, sticker, die-cut, template-cut, stamped or punched letters. See pages 116-117.

LIGNIN-FREE

Paper and paper products that are void of the material (sap) that holds wood fibers together as a tree grows. Most paper is lignin-free except for newsprint, which yellows and becomes brittle with age. Check product labels to be on the safe side. See pages 10 and 24.

MATTING

The act of attaching paper, generally cropped in the shape of a photo, behind the photo to separate it from the scrapbook page's background paper. See pages 55 and 68-69.

MEMORABILIA

Mementos and souvenirs saved from travel, school and life's special events—things that are worthy of remembrance. See pages 97-99

MOUNTING

The process of attaching photos or memorabilia to an album page. Permanent mounting requires the application of adhesive to the back of a photo or mat. Nonpermanent mounting allows you to attach your items to a page and still have the option of easily removing them. See pages 55 and 70.

ORGANIZATION

The act of having pulled or put together ordered photos and memorabilia for the purpose of scrapbooking. Organization of the scrapbook tools and supplies provides for maximum scrapbooking efficiency. See pages 37-38 and 41-51.

PAGE

One side of a scrapbook album—the surface on which you mount photos and memorabilia. Some albums come with pages; some pages are sold separately; some are colored cardstock slipped into a top loader. Buffered, acid- and lignin-free pages are best. See pages 53-75.

PAGE PROTECTORS

Plastic sleeves or pockets that encase finished scrapbook pages for protection. Use only PVC-free protectors. See pages 22-23.

PAGE TITLE

A general or descriptive heading put on a scrapbook page that sums up the theme or essence. Conversely, a "title page" is the first page at the front of the scrapbook, often decorated and embellished (without photos), that describes the book's content. See pages 55, 71 and title page sample on page 117.

PHOTO-SAFE

A term used by companies to indicate that they feel their products are safe to use with photos in a scrapbook album. For archival qualities related to specific materials see page 10.

PIGMENT INK

Pigment inks are water-insoluble and do not penetrate the paper surface. Instead, they adhere to the surface, providing better contrast and clarity. For journaling pens and inkpads,  look for "acid-free" and "photo-safe" on the label. See pages 26 and 35.

POCKET PAGE

A scrapbook page that has been transformed by the addition of a second sheet of cropped paper adhered to the surface, forming a "pocket" in which to place paper memorabilia. See page 99.

PRESERVATION

The act of stabilizing an item from deterioration through the use of proper methods and materials that maintain the conditions and longevity of the item. See pages 97-98.

PUNCHES

Rugged little tools in which you insert a piece of paper, press on the button and out pops a punched shape or design. Punches come in hundreds of shapes and designs and in many sizes. See page 33.

PVC OR POLYVINYL CHLORIDE

A plastic that should not be used in a scrapbook, it emits gases that cause damage to photos. Use only PVC-free plastic page protectors and memorabilia keepers. Safe plastics include polypropylene, poly-ethylene and polyester. See page 10.

SHAPE CUTTERS

Shape blade cutters are made by a number of different companies. They are great for cropping photos, photo mats and journaling blocks into perfect shapes. Shape cutters can cut in circles, ovals and a few other simple shapes. See page 31.

SILHOUETTE

Silhouette cropping entails trimming around the contours of the subject in your photos. When a por-tion of a silhouette-cropped photo's edges have been left intact, it's called a partial silhouette. See page 67.

STAMPS

A wood and rubber tool used to impress a design on paper or cloth; used with a stamp pad or inkpad. With just a few stamps and an inkpad, you can make delicate bor-ders, lacy photo corners, stamped backgrounds, eye-catching photo mats, dressed-up die cuts and jazzy page accents. See page 35.

STICKERS

Gummed with adhesive on one side and a design or pattern on the other, stickers are one of the easiest ways to jazz up scrapbook pages. There are thou-sands of designs to choose from in a multitude of colors, themes and styles—including letter and number, border, journaling and design element stickers. See pages 34 and 107.

TEMPLATES

Templates are stencil-like patterns made of plastic, sturdy paper or cardboard. They can be homemade or purchased and have a multitude of uses. See pages 32 and 107.

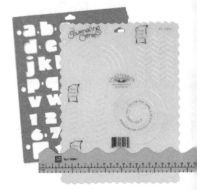

THEME

A theme is the specific subject or topic to which a scrapbook page or an entire scrapbook album is devoted. See pages 82-87.

Additional instructions & credits

Michele Gerbrandt pages featured throughout book:

PAGE 6 THE GERBRANDTS
Decorative scissors (Carl, Platte Productions),
sticker letters (Making Memories), punches
(Family Treasures). Photos Brenda Martinez

PAGE 9 MY NANA'S WEDDING
Background paper (Anna Griffin), journaling
blocks (Anna Griffin), corner punch (Family
Treasures), journaling font (Quark/Bickley Script).

PAGE 13 DANIEL
Pastel papers (Canson). Photo Joyce Feil,
Golden, Colorado

PAGE 13 SASHA KIEV GERBRANDT
Swirl border punch #2 (Family Treasures).

PAGE 16 AS YOU WISH
Papers (Hot Off The Press, Rocky Mountain
Scrapbook Co.), decorative ruler (C-Thru Ruler
Co.), punches (Family Treasures, HyGlo/American
Pin), decorative scissors (Fiskars), die cuts
(Handmade Scraps), journaling template
(EK Success), letter stickers (Bo-Bunny Press),
pen (EK Success).

PAGE 32 LET THE GOOD TIMES ROLL
Oval template and decorative ruler (C-Thru Ruler
Co.), letter template (Frances Meyer), journaling
template (EK Success).

PAGE 40 OUR WEDDING
Border stickers (Mrs. Grossman's Paper Co.).
Photos Greg Baron, Broomhall, Pennsylvania

PAGE 42, 44 A DECADE OF MEMORIES
Papers (Making Memories).

PAGE 52 WHITE FENCE FARM
Patterned paper (Scrappin' Dreams), decorative
scissors (Paper Adventures), corner punch
(McGill), decorative ruler (C-Thru Ruler Co.).

PAGE 59 GREAT SAND DUNES

**PAGES 76-77 ZOO CREW,
THE GERBRANDT FAMILY**
Paper (Making Memories, The Paper Patch), border
stickers (Mrs. Grossman's Paper Co.), journaling
font on title page (Bermuda LP Squiggle).

PAGE 98 TRIP TO FRANCE
Punches (Carl, Family Treasures), memorabilia
pockets (3L Corp.).

PAGE 100 SPECIAL CHRISTMAS MEMORIES
Punches (EK Success), letter stickers (Me & My
Big Ideas).

PAGES 102-103 SASHA'S BIRTHDAY

PAGE 107 DISCOVERY COVE
Title template (EK Success), Bassoon font (DJ
Inkers), stamp (Stampendous!), journaling tem-
plates (C-Thru Ruler Co., EK Success, Staedtler).

PAGE 115 DANIEL'S BIRTHDAY
Patterned paper (Paper Adventures), "happy
birthday" confetti (Amscan), border stickers
(Mrs. Grossman's Paper Co.), title letters (The
Crafter's Workshop).

Other pages, products and photos featured in this book:

PAGE 25 AMANDA
Papers (Bo-Bunny Press, Club Scrap, The
Crafter's Workshop, Ever After, Keeping Memories
Alive, Lasting Impressions, Making Memories,
Paper Fever, Provo Craft, Scrapbook Sally,
Scrappin' Dreams).

PAGE 31 FALL INTO AUTUMN
Patterned paper (Hot Off The Press), NT Circle
Cutter (Lion Office Products), journaling template
(EK Success), Coluzzle® Nested™ Template (Provo
Craft).

PAGE 33 APPLES

Punches used: super jumbo circle, jumbo impatiens leaf, large impatiens leaf, ribbon punches #61001 and #61002, allegro punch (all Emagination Crafts).

PAGE 35 MATTY'S 5TH BIRTHDAY

Stamps: birthday couleur, mon cadeau, patisserie, petite soiree, beaucoup de celebration, imagine circle, breezy birthday, small happy birthday (all Stampendous!) Designs© 2002 Stampendous, Inc.® Rubber Stamps. Brilliance™ (Tsukineko®) inkpad colors: pearlescent lavendar, pearlescent sky blue, pearlescent lime.

PAGE 36 SHANE'S BIRTHDAY

Paper (Canson, The Paper Patch), die cuts (Ellison), silver pen (Sakura).

PAGE 38

12 x 12" paper storage container (Caren's Crafts).

PAGE 48-49

Photos Susan English Photography, Denver, Colorado

PAGES 89-91 MIZZOU

Patterned paper (Embossing Arts), pennant font (Varsity).

PAGE 106

PD fonts (DJ Inkers).

PAGE 107

Journaling stickers (Mrs. Grossman's Paper Co., Sandylion).

PAGE 109 HEAVY METAL GANG

Tooth die cuts (Ellison).

PAGE 112 A GIFT FOR MAX

Patterned paper and stamp (Close To My Heart).

PAGE 116

Left to right: stickers (Making Memories, Westrim Crafts, Mrs. Grossman's Paper Co., S.R.M. Press, K & Co., Sandylion, C-Thru Ruler Co.); templates (Alpha Doodles, C-Thru Ruler Co., C-Thru Ruler Co., EK Success, Frances Meyer, EK Success, The Crafter's Workshop); punches and die cuts (AlphaPics, Accu-Cut, Family Treasures, Creative Trends, Ellison, Westrim Crafts, Deluxe Designs Little Darlings); stamps (Hero Arts, Stampin' Up!, All Night Media, Stampin' Up!, Hero Arts, All Night Media, Rubber Stampede); computer fonts (Comic Sans MS, Juicerman LET, Helvetica, Party LET, PZZ Victorian Swash, Eclectic-1, Hoefler Text).

PAGE 117

Best Friends (Frances Meyer template, Making Memories stickers); Summer Days (AlphaPics die cuts, Hero Arts stamps); Happy Birthday (Family Treasures punches, Sandylion stickers); Our Love Unites Us (PZZ Victorian Swash font, Stampin' Up! Stamps); Our Family (K & Co. stickers, Provo Craft font).

Sources

The following companies manufacture products featured in this book. The companies listed represent a few of the companies that manufacture scrapbook-related products. Please check your local retailers to find these materials. We have made every attempt to properly credit the trademarks and brand names of the items mentioned in this book. We apologize to any company that we have listed or sourced incorrectly.

3L Corp.
(800) 828-3130 (wholesale only)
www.3lcorp.com

3M (888) 364-3577
www.3m.com

Accu-Cut (800) 288-1670
www.accucut.com

American Crafts (800) 879-5185
www.ultimatepens.com

Americn Pin (800) 821-7125
www.americanpin.com

American Tombow
(800) 835-3232
www.tombowusa.com

Amscan, Inc. (800) 444-8887
www.amscan.com

Anna Griffin, Inc. (wholesale
only) (888) 817-8170
www.annagriffin.com

Beadery Craft Products, The
(401) 539-2432
www.thebeadery.com

Bo-Bunny Press
(801) 771-4010 (wholesale only)
www.bobunny.com

Canson, Inc. (800) 628-9283
www.canson-us.com

Caren's Crafts (805) 520-9635

Carl Mfg. USA, Inc.
(847) 956-0730
www.carl-products.com

Carolee's Creations
(435) 563-1100
www.carolees.com

Close to My Heart
(888) 655-6552
www.closetomyheart.com

Club Scrap (888) 634-9100
www.clubscrap.com

Colorbok (800) 366-4660
(wholesale only)
www.colorbok.com

Craf-T Products (507) 235-3996

Crafter's Workshop, The
(914) 345-2838
www.thecraftersworkshop.com

Creative Trends/Pixie Press
(877) 253-7687
www.creativetrends.com

Crop in Style (Platte Productions)
(888) 700-2202
www.cropinstyle.com

C-Thru Ruler Company, The
(800) 243-8419
www.cthruruler.com

Current (877) 665-4458
www.currentcatalog.com

Cut-It-Up (530) 389-2233
www.cut-it-up.com

Deluxe Designs 1-800-96-DELUX
www.deluxecuts.com

Design Originals (800) 877-7820
www.d-originals.com

D.J. Inkers (800) 325-4890
www.djinkers.com

DMD Industries, Inc.
(800) 805-9890
www.dmdind.com

EK Success (800) 524-1349
www.eksuccess.com

Ellison Craft & Design
(800) 253-2238
www.ellison.com

Emagination Crafts, Inc.
(630) 833-9521
www.emaginationcrafts.com

Ever After Scrapbook Company
(800) 646-0010

Ez2cut/Accu-cut (800) 288-1670
www.ez2cut.com

Family Treasures, Inc.
(800) 413-2645
www.familytreasures.com

Fiskars, Inc. (800) 500-4849
www.fiskars.com

Frances Meyer, Inc.
(800) 372-6237
www.francesmeyer.com

Gifted Line, The/Michel & Co.
(800) 533-7263

Hero Arts (800) 822-4379
www.heroarts.com

Hot Off The Press
(800) 227-9595
www.craftpizazz.com
K & Company (888) 244-2083
www.kandcompany.com

Keeping Memories Alive
(800) 419-4949
www.scrapbooks.com

Lasting Impressions for Paper, Inc.
(800) 936-2677

Lion Office Products (800) 421-1848
www.lionop.com

Making Memories (800) 286-5263
www.makingmemories.com

Marvy Uchida (800) 541-5877
www.uchida.com

McGill Inc. (800) 982-9884
www.mcgillinc.com

Me and My BIG Ideas
(949) 589-4607 (wholesale only)
www.meandmybigideas.com

Mrs. Grossman's Paper Co.
(800) 429-5459
www.mrsgrossmans.com

Northern Spy (530) 620-7430
www.northernspy.com

NRN Designs (wholesale only)
(800) 421-6958
www.nrndesigns.com

Paper Adventures (800) 727-0699
www.paperadventures.com

Paper Patch, The (800) 397-2737
(wholesale only)
www.paperpantry.com

Plaid Enterprises, Inc.
(800) 842-4197
www.plaidenterprises.com

Preservation Technologies, L.P.
(800) 416-2665
www.ptlp.com

Provo Craft (800) 937-7686
www.provocraft.com

PSX Design (Duncan Enterprises)
(800) 438-6226
www.psxdesign.com

Punch Bunch, The
(254)791-4209 (wholesale only)
www.thepunchbunch.com

PM Designs (formerly Puzzle Mates)
(888) 595-2887
www.puzzlemates.com

Ranger Industries, Inc.
(800) 244-2211
www.rangerink.com

Rocky Mountain Scrapbook Co.
(801) 796-1471

Rubber Stampede (800) 423-4135
www.rubberstampede.com

Rupert, Gibbon & Spider Inc.
(Jacquard Products)
(800) 442-0455
www.jacquardproducts.com

Sakura of America (800) 776-6257
www.sakuraofamerica.com

Sandylion Sticker Designs
(800) 387-4215
www.sandylion.com

Scrapbook Sally (86) SBSally
www.scrapbooksally.com

Scrappin' Dreams (417) 831-1882
www.scrappindreams.com

SRM Press, Inc. (800) 323-9589
www.srmpress.com

Staedtler, Inc. (800) 927-7723
www.staedtler-usa.com

Stampendous! (wholesale only)
(800) 869-0474
www.stampendous.com

Stampin' Up! (800) 782-6787
www.stampinup.com

Starry Night Creations
(612) 799-1416
www.starrynightcreations.com

StenSource International, Inc.
(800) 642-9293
www.stensource.com

Stickopotamus (888) 270-4443

Suzy's Zoo (619) 282-9401
www.suzyszoo.com

Tsukineko, Inc. (800) 769-6633
www.tsukineko.com

un-du Products, Inc. (888) 289-8638

Westrim Crafts (800) 727-2727
www.westrimcrafts.com

Wubie Prints (888) 256-0107
www.wubieprints.com

Xyron (800) 793-3523
www.xyron.com

Index